Bob Polunsky's
FLICKER FOOTNOTES

by

Bob Polunsky

DORRANCE PUBLISHING CO., INC.
PITTSBURGH, PENNSYLVANIA 15222

All Rights Reserved
Copyright © 2003 by Bob Polunsky
No part of this book may be reproduced or transmitted
in any form or by any means, electronic or mechanical,
including photocopying, recording, or by any information
storage and retrieval system without permission in
writing from the publisher.

ISBN # 0-8059-6145-3
Printed in the United States of America

First Printing

For information or to order additional books, please write:
Dorrance Publishing Co., Inc.
701 Smithfield Street
Third Floor
Pittsburgh, Pennsylvania 15222
U.S.A.
1-800-788-7654
Or visit our web site and on-line catalog at www.dorrancepublishing.com

To Paul Markey with gratitude for his encouragement and friendship.

Contents

Introduction vii

1. Texas Is Really a Suburb of Hollywood .1
2. At Home with the Duke 8
3. The Inimitable Barbra Streisand 13
4. Blonde Bombshell Smacks Polunsky (and It Made the Papers!) 19
5. Jane Withers Lassoed a Career 23
6. Olivia, 2; Joan, 1 27
7. Pia's Polack 32
8. George Burns, a Legend in His Own Time 39
9. Robert Duvall, an Actor's Actor 50
10. Hello, Dolly! 54
11. Macho Clint Eastwood 58
12. Best of the Bonds 61
13. The Junket from Hell 64
14. Shhhh! Melanie Has a Man in Her Room! 67
15. Rodney Dangerfield Gets Respect 71

16. Cruising Down the Caribbean with Lenny 73

17. Hollywood's Professor Henry Higgins 76

18. Bagging Bagger Vance with Bruce 78

19. You Ain't Seen Nothin' Yet! 80

20. Cameos—the Women 84
    Genevieve Bujold, Sandy Dennis, Dorothy Lamour, Ginger Rogers, Margot Kidder, Tina Turner, Sylvia Miles, Madonna, Shirley MacLaine, Bette Midler, Shelley Long, Olympia Dukakis, Julia Roberts, Barbara Stanwyck, Sonja Henie, Rosie O'Donnell, Lana Turner, Meryl Streep, Kathleen Turner, Sharon Stone, Jodie Foster, Kathy Grant, Carol Channing, Lena Horne, Pearl Bailey, Marianna Blase

21. Cameos—the Men 93
    Vincent Price, Cary Grant, John Lithgow, Ned Beatty, Christian Slater, James Woods, Richard Dreyfuss, Paul Mazursky, Spike Lee, Roman Polanski, Benny Goodman, Bill Murray, Dan Aykroyd, John Belushi, Andrew Dice Clay, Mickey Rooney, Danny Kaye, Yul Brynner, William Holden, Ernest Borgnine, Jack Benny, Peter Ustinov, Jan Murray, John Malkovich, Steve Guttenberg, Steven Spielberg, James Caan, Danny Glover, Samuel L. Jackson, John Cusack, Johnny Depp, Jack Lemmon, Walter Matthau, Pat O'Brien, Roddy McDowall, Christopher Reeve, Eddie Murphy, Christopher Lambert, Chris Farley, David Spade, Franc Roddam, Robert Morley, Tom Cruise, Sean Penn, Robin Williams, Fred Astaire, Gene Kelly, John Goodman

22. I'll Always Remember Pearl Harbor 101

INTRODUCTION

When I was an infant my mother took me to the movies with her because she couldn't find a babysitter. It was during the Depression years and I'm sure she couldn't afford a babysitter so she resourcefully found a way of seeing her movie and taking care of me at the same time. She wrapped me in swaddling clothes, probably crossed her fingers in hopes I wouldn't cry, then bought a ticket to see Johnny Weissmuller in "Tarzan, the Ape Man." It was Weissmuller's first "Tarzan" movie, and Mom was a fan of the comic strip. She later told me I slept all the way through it, and that sounded like treason to a born movie lover. As hard as it is to believe, I caught the show biz "bug" around the time that Tarzan was swinging on jungle vines in "Tarzan, the Ape Man."

The movie came out in 1932, when I was one year old. As soon as I could walk and talk, I became a movie fanatic and went to every show I could. Movies were so important to me that I would ask my parents or grandparents for a dime just to see a show. I must have been pretty persuasive because I usually got the price of admission. Looking back, I sometimes think they were glad to get rid of me, but they opened a whole new world and I was supremely grateful.

I was about four years old when I saw "Valiant Is the Word for Carrie" at the Texas Theater in downtown San Antonio. I can still picture Carrie (Gladys George) behind bars in one of her more melodramatic scenes of a movie that would be rated "R" today. It just wasn't meant for kids to see a movie about a woman who felt duty-bound to care for orphans. But it was another movie my mom wanted to see and, again, there was no one to leave me with.

The first all-out child's movie I remember was "Snow White and the Seven Dwarfs" at the Majestic. I saw it with my cousins and our mothers, and we vowed to see every cartoon movie we could after that. I kept that vow and am still keeping it when it comes to Disney's animated films. I don't let any of them get by me.

I've seen movies evolve from Hollywood tinsel to modern-day grit. Of course, that kind of realism doesn't make a pretty picture, but—when they are well-acted and smoothly directed—they can be fascinating!

Bob Polunsky

Some of the top stars of the 1930s specialized in gritty realism, and they included Paul Muni, Bette Davis, Gable, Tracy, Bogart, William Powell, Ronald Colman, Margaret Sullavan, and Myrna Loy. I never met any of them, but I sure wanted to. I didn't meet any stars until I was grown, and few of them filled the shoes of Muni, Davis, Gable, or Bogart. But some did, and I made up for lost time by interviewing as many as I could.

I've wanted to be involved with the movie industry in some way ever since, but it wasn't easy to do. I couldn't become a "movie star" even though my friends used to tell me I looked like Lew Ayres, the "Dr. Kildare" of Hollywood. Even if I did look like Lew Ayres, I was too self-conscious to act in school plays. But somehow, some way, I was going to be part of the movie business. I was obsessed with the idea even though I didn't fully understand why.

Thinking about it now, I wonder if it was just an obsessive desire to get attention. It couldn't be escapism, because I had a great family life and my parents encouraged me to plan for the future. They didn't pay much attention to my grandiose ideas of show business, though. Dad wanted me to study Law. Mom wanted me to be a concert pianist and follow in her footsteps because she was the Concertmaster of the San Antonio Symphony at the time.

She thought I would make a good concert pianist because I had taught myself the rudiments while listening to the piano teacher give my sister, Dottie, a lesson. I taught myself well enough to give a concert at the San Pedro Playhouse when I was thirteen. But it wasn't what I wanted. I wanted to meet the people who put glamour in the world, and finally got that chance when I graduated from college.

My first interview with a movie star was strictly by accident, but it whetted my appetite. It was in 1953, when I worked at KABC radio in San Antonio. I got the job of Traffic Manager right after graduation from the University of Texas at Austin. It wasn't a glamorous job, but it was a foot in the door.

Some stars from Hollywood came to San Antonio to promote their movies and stage shows, and the station had a woman on the staff who interviewed them. Her name was Monette Shaw, and she asked me to go with her when Tyrone Power and Raymond Massey were in town doing readings from "John Brown's Body" at the Municipal Auditorium. Monette knew I was starstruck. Besides, she needed someone to carry her Wollensack, the heavy tape recorder she used for interviews.

Unfortunately, she couldn't get the recorder to work when we met the stars in their room at the Robert E. Lee Hotel. While she tampered with it, I talked to them about their show and their careers. The next day Monette had me as her guest on her daily radio show so I could talk to her about the things Power and Massey had talked to me about.

In time, I went into the Sales Department to make a living but kept doing interviews with stars as the occasions presented themselves. I finally had my taste of show business and I loved it, even if it was nothing more than a hobby, and I didn't get paid for any of it for the first couple of years. I started getting paid when KITE-FM hired me to do a daily review on radio in 1966. The reviews would be sponsored by the San Antonio Motion Picture Association, an organization of the various chains of theaters created to do joint advertising. My program was their first venture, and it lasted on the same station for twenty-one years. Afterwards I moved to WOAI radio to do a weekly program of movie trivia along with movie reviews. I'm still at that station doing virtually the same thing fifteen years later. The only difference is that my reviews air daily and the trivia program is weekly.

Interviewing stars and reviewing movies developed into a full-time career. Some interviews were planned. Others were spontaneous, to take advantage of an opportunity. To make sure we (I had gotten married in the meantime) would always have food on the table, I kept my day job of advertising sales along with my interviewing and reviewing. It wasn't hard. I much preferred talking to movie stars than sleeping or eating, and some of my impromptu interviews got started in genuinely funny ways while I was out of town on weekends to take part in movie press junkets.

For example, I had a run-in (literally) with Roman Polanski at a Hollywood restaurant and wrote about it for the *San Antonio Light*. I yelled across a dance floor at a Chicago hotel to get Carol Burnett's attention and a chance to talk to her. Our interview got a plug on the front page of the *Light*. I had a chance meeting with Dana Andrews in the lobby of the Beverly Wilshire Hotel in Beverly Hills and a short impromptu meeting with Tom Bosely in the Regency Hotel restaurant in New York. I considered each occasion a valid interview and found a way of talking about it on radio, in print, and on TV.

Many of the radio and TV interviews became newspaper interviews. I was at the *Light* for sixteen years, then at the *Express* for another sixteen years before joining the staff of Primetime Newspapers, a syndicate that operates twenty-one papers in South Texas.

My TV career started in earnest in 1968 with a program called "Footnotes on the Flickers" on KONO-TV, the ABC affiliate in San Antonio. When I moved to KENS-TV. the CBS affiliate, I changed the name to plain "Flicker Footnotes" and used it as an umbrella title for all my activities in radio, TV, and print.

While at KENS I was asked to put my reviews and interviews on the CBS Southwest Regional News satellite. It meant they would be seen in small towns that did not have official movie critics in the electronic media. I actually covered more than the Southwest, as I received mail from New Orleans; Augusta, Georgia; Jacksonville, Florida; Chicago; Mexico City; and even one letter from Guam. This satellite activity gave me a chance to expand my coverage of reviews and interviews.

Bob Polunsky

I've had a long career, starting with radio and TV in 1953, and was the first movie critic on both mediums in Texas. I've stayed on both mediums—as well as in print—ever since. This year (2003) is my fiftieth year in the media, and I'm still at it.

Over the years I've met Cary Grant, Sean Connery, Barbra Streisand, Clint Eastwood, Olivia DeHavilland, Gregory Peck, Harrison Ford, Robert Downey, Jr., Steven Spielberg, Spike Lee, Martin Scorsese, Lena Horne, Carol Channing, Pearl Bailey, Lillian Gish, Sharon Stone, Paul Newman, Robert Redford, Tina Turner, Lana Turner, Claire Trevor, Jane Greer, Dorothy Lamour, Sissy Spacek, Kathleen Turner, Glenn Close, Jill Clayburgh, Madonna, Sean Penn, Jessica Lange, Dustin Hoffman, John Wayne, Ben Affleck, Matt Damon, Barbara Rush, Robin Williams, Danny DeVito, Michael Douglas, Burt Lancaster, Kirk Douglas, Burt Reynolds, Dinah Shore, and hundreds more. Some remembered me when I saw them a second time, like Gary Burghoff (TV's "Radar" in "M.A.S.H."). I interviewed him when he came to San Antonio to be in a play at the Fiesta Dinner Playhouse. The next time he came, he asked that I be the one from the newspaper to interview him.

The point is, I had fun trying to find out what made them tick. Our interviews were intended to be part of the publicity for specific movies, so many of them were just fluff stuff to please the studios. But not all of them. It was more fun trying to find out what the person was really like. Some responded well, and—for that day anyway—we became friends.

Chita Rivera summed up the feeling of exhilaration that I had when doing an interview. She would say, "I've found a new friend!"—then she would sigh. I always feel like doing the same thing. It was when Dolly Parton sat on my lap for our interview and when Ann Jillian planted a kiss on my cheek after an interview and when Tina Turner sang to me as part of our interview and when Natalie Wood said she always liked to talk to men named "Bob" (she was Mrs. Bob Wagner in private life).

Jan Murray asked me to give him a tour of San Antonio movie houses. Gary Busey wanted me to interview him while he toured the Alamo. Steve Guttenberg called the video store my wife and I owned to see if we could get a copy of one of his early movies. Robert Redford called me at home to ask if I would help promote a documentary he had just made. Sissy Spacek saw me with my wife and daughters at a hotel restaurant and came to our table. I had interviewed her the day before and she remembered me and wanted to meet my family. It was a friendly act that she didn't have to do. It also revealed something about her character as well as her personality.

Talking to the stars helped me understand what they were all about. It was an ego trip for me—because I was with a celebrity—and for them because they were "stars" in the spotlight. It was also satisfying for me to break through the tinsel and find the real person underneath. Patrick Swayze paid me a terrific compliment after one interview. He said he liked talking to me because I looked him in the eye so he felt I was actually interested in what he had to say.

Patrick Swayze provided one of my favorite "Flicker Footnotes." The following are some more of them. There aren't the only footnotes I've had on the flickers over the years. But they are the most memorable ones.

1.
TEXAS IS REALLY A SUBURB OF HOLLYWOOD

THE IDEA OF A TEXAN WRITING ABOUT BIG-TIME, NATIONALLY FAMOUS MOVIE stars may sound out of place, but it isn't. I went to Hollywood, New York, and everywhere the stars gathered to promote their films during my interview years between 1953 and 2001. I met and talked to as many as I could and found some who were down to earth and friendly. Sure, some were condescending, because they were like people everywhere. But every time I wrote about them in the newspaper or talked about them on the radio and tv, people would ask me if movie stars I meet are much different from us "home folks" in Texas. My answer is always the same: Hell, no! Most of them were from Texas anyway.

Saying "most of them" may be stretching the truth, but a lot of Texans migrate to Hollywood and make it big in show business. The native-born Texas movie stars come from every nook and cranny in the state. Some—like Patrick Swayze, Joan Crawford, Brenda Vacarro, and Ann Sheridan—are from the state's biggest towns. Others—like Carolyn Jones, Powers Boothe, writer-director Robert Benton, Farrah Fawcett, and Chill Wills—are from smaller towns. The towns may be forgotten, but the celebrities are remembered.

My fellow San Antonians include Carol Burnett, the one and only successful female clown in show business today. She was born and raised (until the age of twelve, anyway) in San Antonio, and I've seen her old house on Commerce near Zarzamora Street. I've talked to her at length about her San Antonio roots, and she told me she "learned" the movie business from her grandfather when he managed the old State Theater on Main Avenue. I remember her telling me she would go to the movies every waking moment if she could, and her grandfather would help her. The State was a sub-run movie house just north of the downtown area. They changed programs a couple of times a week, and they always brought back the "big ones" from first-run engagements at the Majestic, Aztec, Texas, and Empire Theaters.

The State was originally called the Majestic and was the flagship of the Hoblitzelle movie chain. It was also a vaudeville house at one time, and I remember walking over the grounds where the State had stood before it was torn down. I was with Bob Hope at the time. He wanted to find the location of his dressing room when he played the State.

Hope came to San Antonio during Hemisfair, our World's Fair in 1968. He was one of many visitors, and I was surprised to find how many of them had either lived in San Antonio or earnestly wanted to. They all had something nice to say about our Riverwalk (built for Hemisfair) and the winding San Antonio River that had so many twists as it flowed through downtown San Antonio.

When Carol Burnett visited The Alamo City, she took time to attend a public school meeting of some kind. It was at her former grade school, and I had a nice chat with her at the meeting.

The next time we met was in Chicago for a big bash celebrating the release of "A Wedding" with Burnett as its star. We were having press conferences the day after the party, and that meant no individual press interviews. I was determined to get one with Carol Burnett, so—when I saw her talking to a group of reporters at the party—I yelled across the dance floor, saying, "Hey, are you the one from San Antonio?"

She stopped in mid-sentence and yelled back, "Who's talking about San Antonio?"

I identified myself, and she came over to me for a nice, long, friendly interview. I put it in the paper intact and got a call from the studio thanking me for the publicity.

Unfortunately, Carol Burnett doesn't make a lot of movies. But I've seen all of them no matter how few or how many. She is at the top of my San Antonio list and always will be.

Other stars from San Antonio include Bruce McGill, my Movie Cruise buddy and a friend of long standing. He was born and raised in San Antonio and is always recognized when he comes home to visit his mother, the artist Adriel McGill.

Joan Crawford moved away from San Antonio shortly after she was born. Her name was then Lucille LeSeur. When she moved to Kansas City, she was known as Billie Cassin. Then she moved to Hollywood and the star named Joan Crawford was born. She had one of the longest careers in Hollywood but wasn't considered a versatile actress until she changed from bitchy characters to sympathetic ones. She got audience sympathy for her performance in "Mildred Pierce" and earned an Oscar for it.

I don't think she thought of Hollywood as "home" because she often referred to her "home town" of San Antonio in TV interviews. She even came back to San Antonio to meet with the Pepsi Cola Board of Directors when she was its chairperson. She didn't make many friends for Pepsi Cola or for herself when she discouraged newspaper reporters from asking questions. One newsperson retaliated by writing a story without talking to Miss Crawford, and her headline caused a minor ruckus. It said, "Joan Crawford visits her home town of San Antonio for the first time in 50 years!"

Bob Polunsky's Flicker Footnotes

The end result was that San Antonio-born Joan Crawford never came back to her home town.

Pedro Gonzalez-Gonzalez is also from the Alamo City and frequently comes back to urge City Council members to name a downtown park after him. Pedro wants recognition and he really hasn't had much of it since his John Wayne movie days. The Duke "discovered" him when he was doing a talk show on WOAI Radio and hired him for "The High and the Mighty" as well as other Wayne features.

George Strait is from San Antonio. We met at the airport once when he came over to me in the Baggage Area to tell me he watches my reviews on TV.

Ann Harding, the sophisticated star of stage and screen in the 1930s, was born at Fort Sam Houston, Texas, and Fort Sam is part of San Antonio. She always spoke favorably of San Antonio during her career. So did character actress Florence Bates, the San Antonio native who played Mrs. Van Hopper in "Rebecca."

Dorothy Dell was a pretty starlet from San Antonio who costarred with Shirley Temple in "Little Miss Marker" in 1934. A car wreck snuffed out her life and put an end to her promising career.

One-time child star Henry Thomas wasn't exactly from San Antonio but he called San Antonio "home." He was raised on a ranch between San Antonio and Floresville, attending schools in both cities. Once he was "discovered" by Steven Spielberg to star in "E.T.: The Extra-Terrestrial," he called himself a native San Antonian. He grew up on the screen, appearing with some of Hollywood's more outstanding adult stars. They included Brad Pitt in "Legends of the Fall," Gene Hackman in "Misunderstood," and Annette Bening in "Valmont."

He filmed several movies in Texas, most notably "Cloak and Dagger" with Dabney Coleman in San Antonio and "Raggedy Man" with Sissy Spacek in San Marcos and Buda. I remember visiting him on a plane from Los Angeles to San Antonio. We sat next to one another and had an enjoyable conversation en route to the Alamo City.

I later saw him when he was active in his rock band in San Antonio. He's a shy guy who needs a script to help him develop his personality. Once he gets his teeth into a role, he's a darned good little actor.

Dabney Coleman often visits his brother in San Antonio. Both are Austin natives, and, after all, Austin is only a hop, skip, and a jump (70 miles) from San Antonio.

Then there are those expatriates from other states who call San Antonio "home" for a time. Pola Negri is probably the most famous. The Polish-born silent screen star inherited a wealthy mansion in San Antonio and spent her last years there. She rarely went out in public without a large hat and sunglasses to make herself inconspicuous. At least in her mind.

Bob Polunsky

I saw her several times because our friends, Bob and Maggie Sheerin, had her at their annual New Year's Eve party. Ms. Negri always thought it was to celebrate her birthday, which was on December 31. She was quite colorful and interesting, and there was always a crowd around her at the Sheerins' parties.

Bobby Sheerin wore a tux to his party and urged his friends to do the same. I remember standing next to Pola Negri when she stopped, turned to face me and—because of her failing eyesight—thought I was a uniformed waiter.

"More shom-pane, boy," she said, holding out her glass, which I dutifully took and refilled.

Ms. Negri was very vain. If anyone made mention of her career she would start a lengthy conversation about pictures she had made. "Did you see me in 'Barbed Wire'?" she would ask or maybe sing a few bars from her sexy song hit, "Paradise" (which was banned from the air waves for being too suggestive).

She couldn't see clearly but refused to wear glasses. She also wore her hair in the same style that she wore in her silent movies. Her hair (probably a wig) was coal black and shiny. Her sleeves were long enough to hide her wrinkles, and she always wore black to make herself look thinner.

Actually she was very petite, and—even at her advanced age—looked sexy. Pola Negri stories would circulate fast in our group. Some talked knowingly about Ms. Negri's "engagement" to Rudolf Valentino, although there has never been any proof of their relationship.

The story that was told most often was that when she went into Campbell's Funeral Home in New York City to view the body, she swooned in a dramatic way. When one of the reporters with a flashbulb muttered that he didn't get that picture, Ms. Negri got up and swooned again. This scene was restaged in "Valentino," the second movie biography of the Latin Lover. Leslie Caron did the swooning and her character had a fictitious name. Pola Negri refused to grant permission to use her name.

Toward the end of her life, Ms. Negri made appearances at Trinity University and St. Mary's University when she left collections of her films to them. She was also the official "hostess" for our Hemisfair in 1968 and greeted visitors to the Alamo City for that World's Fair. At the time, she referred to herself as "a San Antonian."

Tommy Lee Jones was married to a San Antonio woman and lived in San Antonio while he was married. He kept an apartment here after his divorce, staying in San Antonio between visits to his West Texas ranch. Actually, Tommy Lee was born in Texas, but not in San Antonio. Today he still calls the Alamo City his home.

Bob Burke Easton is a dialogue coach for the stars and usually has a small role in his clients' movies. He was born in Chicago, where he was a Quiz Kid before he was twelve. He moved to San Antonio during his days in high school, where he was a whiz at math. We became good friends (he was a great help with math problems), and I asked him to co-host a movie cruise with me during the 1980s. More about Bob's San Antonio years in the chapter about him.

Olivia de Havilland had a home at Medina Lake near San Antonio for a few years. Her children attended the University of Texas at Austin, and she would spend many months of every year in the Alamo City. But she rarely ventured out in public. She stayed close to her home at Medina Lake.

Clark Gable—who was one of Olivia's "Gone with the Wind" co-stars—was from Ohio, but he had a ranch near Ingram, Texas, not far from San Antonio. It was when he was married to Houston socialite Rhea Langham during the 1930s. They had a large gate at the long entranceway to their ranch, with the words, "House of the Two Gables," on the top of that gate. It was left standing as a tourist attraction after the Gables split. I've seen the gate, and so have thousands of others.

Opera singer Dorothy Kirsten made San Antonio her home base during her most active years. She was often seen at social gatherings and was consistently in the news for her activities with San Antonio charities.

Lupe Velez, aka "The Mexican Spitfire," was from Mexico but was educated at a San Antonio convent. She rarely came back after she settled in Hollywood, however. Her scandalous suicide almost erased her name from the list of notable Hollywood personalities. But for a time at least, Lupe Velez was a San Antonian.

So was Audie Murphy, aka the most decorated hero of World War II. Murphy was actually born in the small town of Kingston, Texas, but he received much of his military training at Fort Sam Houston. The Audie Murphy Hospital, a veterans' hospital named in his honor, is located in San Antonio.

Darla Hood, the tiny "leading lady" of the "Our Gang" ("Little Rascals") featurettes, lived in San Antonio for a while. She always called California her home but went to school in San Antonio when she "outgrew" those "Little Rascals." Barbara Pittenger—a classmate of mine from grade school through high school—was her cousin. Darla died in 2002. She was 71 years old and a recluse. Her death on February 24 was not listed in the San Antonio newspaper until March 15.

John Schneider—star of TV's "The Dukes of Hazzard" as well as many Hollywood films—was once a San Antonio resident. He also resided in Houston for a while, but—according to everything he told me in his interview—he had a fondness for San Antonio.

Actress Brenda Marshall was Errol Flynn's costar in "The Sea Hawk" and "Footsteps in the Dark." She was a dark beauty who would have had a major screen career had she not retired to marry William Holden.

Brenda was originally from the Philippines, and her father was in the military. He was stationed in San Antonio during her teenage years when she attended Alamo Heights High School.

Writer-director Oliver Stone was married to a San Antonian and lived in the Alamo City as long as his marriage lasted. Unfortunately, that wasn't too long. Stone is a good interview and was always available whenever he lived in the Alamo City. He and I had some good times talking about politics. He was very outspoken in his views and incorporated them into his movie, "JFK." He was much more blunt about JFK's assassination and its political overtones than he was about Nixon's scandalous times in the White House in his movie called "Nixon." I remember asking him why he didn't make a movie about LBJ. "You could even call it that, and everyone would know exactly how you feel about the man," I asked him. His reply was a simple "Hmmmm. Not a bad idea." But he never made that movie.

Some of Hollywood's brightest stars came from Dallas, Texas. They include sultry, glamorous Linda Darnell, star of many Tyrone Power adventures, and husky-voiced Ann Sheridan, star of many of James Cagney's gangster pictures.

The composer-lyricist team of Harvey Schmidt and Tom Jones ("I Do, I Do," "The Fantasticks") were both from the Dallas area.

Comedian King Donovan (aka Mr. Imogene Coca when married to her) was from Dallas. So were Doris Roberts, Mary Anne Edwards (who had a strong featured role in "Giant"), Tess Harper, Oscar winner Marcia Gay Harden, Helen Shaver, one-time child star Robby Benson, and James Hall, one of Jean Harlow's costars in "Hell's Angels."

John Boles, one of Hollywood's early heartthrobs, was from a small town near Dallas, and Greer Garson called Dallas her home when she was married to oil man Buddy Fogelson.

Owen Wilson, Jackie Chan's costar in "Shanghai Noon," is from Dallas, along with his two brothers, who also act in Hollywood films.

Sissy Spacek and her cousin, Rip Torn, are from Quitman, near Dallas, and Ginger Rogers won a Charleston contest in Dallas (but she was living in Fort Worth at the time). Ginger called herself a Texan because her mother was the Drama Critic for the Fort Worth Star Telegram and they made their home in Fort Worth for a number of years.

Mary Martin was from Weatherford, a small town on the other side of Fort Worth, and Ruta Lee is from Fort Worth proper. She goes back as often as she can to appear in a play at the Casa Manana Playhouse. Bill Paxton is another Fort Worther, and he also mentions his home town in his interviews.

Houston is another city known for its access to Hollywood. Gale Storm won a movie contract in a contest in her hometown of Houston, and Kathryn Grandstaff (her movie name was Kathy Grant before she married Bing Crosby) was born in Houston.

Ann Miller is from Chirena, a small town near Houston. Patrick Swayze was born in Houston, where his mother taught dancing. Patrick is her most famous student.

Renee Zellweger is from Katy, just outside of Houston, and the Quaid brothers—Randy and Dennis—are from Houston itself.

Famed director King Vidor came from Galveston, which is about fifty miles south of Houston. Evelyn Keyes is from Port Arthur, which is about fifty miles north of Houston.

Hedy Lamarr and Gene Tierney lived in Houston when they were married to oil men who operated out of there. Writer Horton Foote is from Wharton, which is about a hundred miles southwest of Houston.

Austin has been home to many stars, most notably Zachary Scott and Willie Nelson. A theater is named in Scott's honor. It's on Sixth Street, and is the hub of local theatrical production. Willie Nelson's name is synonymous with Austin because of his many concerts.

Dana Andrews and his brother, Steve Forrest, claimed Austin as their home town. So did character actor Pat Hingle when he was a student at the University of Texas. Matthew McConnaughy is a Longview native who appeared in most of Austinite writer-director Richard Linklater's movies.

Ethan Hawke was born in Austin and came back to make "The Newton Boys" for Linklater.

Sandra Bullock isn't from Austin but has a home there. Madeline Stowe lives in Fredericksburg with her Texas-born TV star husband, Brian Benben. Fredericksburg is about fifty miles from both San Antonio and Austin.

Comedian Steve Martin hails from Waco, a city between Austin and Dallas, and glamorous dancer Cyd Charisse is from Amarillo in the Texas Panhandle. Amarillo is about as far from the major Texas cities as El Paso is, and El Paso is Debbie Reynolds's home town.

Singer Buddy Holly was from Lubbock. He was flying home in a snowstorm along with fellow performers Richie Valens (another Texan) and the Big Bopper when the plane crashed. Holly made Lubbock famous long before Gary Busey (another Texan) portrayed him on the screen. Lubbock is a comparatively small Texas town, but not nearly as small as some Texas towns that were home towns to stars like Gene Autry (from Tioga), Dale Evans (from Uvalde), and Lenny Von Dohlen (from Goliad). Lenny was the first movie personality I asked to cohost movie cruises with me during the 1980s. We've been good friends ever since. Like many other stars born in Texas or moving there of their own accord, Lenny was what we in Texas call "home folks."

2.
AT HOME WITH THE DUKE

THE FIRST TIME I MET JOHN WAYNE WAS AT THE OPENING OF THE MARRIOTT Airport Hotel by the Los Angeles Airport. Virtually everybody who was anybody in Hollywood was there, but the Duke was the one I wanted to see.

The second time I met him was when Carl Ferrazza, the manager of Field Operations for the United Artists studio, called to invite me to have dinner with John Wayne at his home in Newport Beach, California. To use Carl's words, "John Wayne would like an opportunity to talk to you about his newest film, 'Brannigan.' It was made in England and is different from anything else he's done. Will you be able to come?" I assured him I would, and he said he would put a first-class airplane ticket in the mail that very day.

It would be impossible to turn Carl down for anything he asked. Carl Ferrazza at United Artists and Stu Gottesman at Warner Brothers were two of a kind in that regard, as they were virtually the only field reps who showed a concern and consideration for reporters. Both were pros in every sense of the word so they knew how to make press people feel good about the job we had to do. Neither Carl nor Stu ever acted as if we had to do anything. It was a professional thing, not a personal one. But press people loved doing things to help promote movies for Carl and Stu.

But I'm getting ahead of myself. The meeting at the Marriott is forever engraved on my brain for one simple reason: John Wayne thought autographs were silly, so he found a way around them. When I saw him at the hotel opening, I went over to the table to ask for an autograph even though my wife told me not to. "Why bother the man?" she said. But I wanted that autograph. I went up to him, and he responded in a typical fashion.

"Why, sure," he said, as he pulled out a stack of business cards from his pocket. He had already scribbled his name on each card so we would have the printed name of "John Wayne," and, underneath it or above it, his hand-scribbled name. It was a memorable way to give out an autograph, and I found out later that he always carried those signed business cards with him.

Why no one else at the hotel opening thought of doing the same thing, I don't know. They all made a big production out of signing their names on a program or napkin or whatever was handy. A collector of autographs would have a field day because such Hollywood luminaries as Ann Blyth (looking radiant in her form-fitting dress) was there, as were Harry James and his Band and Bob Crosby and his Bobcats (I got autographs from both but promptly lost them. John Wayne's autograph is still safely in my drawer).

I remember seeing Eva Gabor there and listening to her laugh. She looked as if she were poured into her dress and seemed proud of it. Fellow Texan Ann Miller was there, but she acted as if she didn't want to meet anyone. Rosalind Russell was there. I recognized her by her laugh, not her looks. Her face looked puffy because of the cortisone she was taking, but it was her, all right.

The star-studded affair was to celebrate the hotel opening, and I wondered why I was invited. When the agent (Fran Wise from Levenson and Hill) called, I asked what I could possibly do.

"This hotel has everything...I mean everything," she answered. "They even have swim-up bar, so mention it in your column. That's all they expect."

They put on quite a spread for just a mention. Tables piled high with food, a day in the swimming pool, and a two-hour press conference with Marriott officials, to name just a few things. But it was the big bash with all the stars that got most of our attention, and I filled my column with star names although I didn't have much of a chance to talk with them. The closest I came to it was a brief comment to Rosalind Russell when she caught me staring at her.

"Can I help you?" she asked, and I responded quickly, "Aren't you Rosalind Russell?"

When she answered, "Yes," I just told her I much I enjoyed her movies.

That was in 1971. I was in Hollywood every month that year—sometimes more than once a month—but I didn't get the invitation to have dinner with John Wayne until 1975.

The trip was a little troublesome. I took the plane to LAX, then hopped the bus for Newport Beach, then took a cab from the bus stop to John Wayne's home. His address had been furnished, and I was welcomed with open arms. The Duke himself came to the door.

It's a nice house that borders the waterfront. The Duke explained that he had a boat ready to go whenever he wanted and his sons, Pat and Michael, often joined him.

We went in and had drinks. The Duke preferred tequila straight from the bottle. Then he told me to help myself from the buffet and let him know when I'm ready for a tour of the house. I noticed that he took the bottle with him when he left the room.

In the course of the visit we talked only briefly about "Brannigan." The studio had sent a print to San Antonio so I could see it before I made the trip. It was an interesting movie with Wayne as a two-fisted cop. He played the character the same way he played a cowboy in his films.

Brannigan is a Chicago cop who goes to London to find an American criminal. Much of the entertainment was watching all-American John Wayne try to fit the mold of a British cop. He insisted on doing things his way, whether it was brawling in a pub or tracking down clues. Some of it was funny and all of it was good, with a stellar cast supporting the Duke.

Richard Attenborough, Mel Ferrer, John Vernon, Ralph Meeker, and two very pretty English girls (Lesley-Anne Down and Judy Geeson) were in the cast, but the Duke overshadowed them the same way he overshadowed Hollywood actors in his movies. His walk called attention to itself, his drawl was unmistakably Hollywoodese, and his steely-eyed look told his antagonist that he wasn't going to take any guff off of him. It was all pleasantly done, as far as the English were concerned. The Duke added enough two-fisted American action to make the movie move.

We talked briefly about the movie in the Duke's backyard "port." That being done, we went back into the house for "the tour," and what a tour it was. I got off on the wrong foot, though, because I told Wayne that Big John Hamilton from San Antonio sent his regards.

"Oh, my God! Don't tell him you were here, for God's sakes. He'll drive me crazy wanting to know why he wasn't invited!"

Big John was a San Antonio groupie who followed macho stars around like a puppy. He always invited John Wayne to his "parties"—which were really more like orgies—and he always let all of San Antonio know that "the Duke was at my house last night." He would tell customers who visited Big John's Steakhouse on the Austin Highway. It was Big John's way of entertaining them, and they lapped it up.

John Wayne's didn't go to all Big John's parties, but Big John made it sound as if he did. Hamilton also invited Clint Eastwood and a few fellow groupies. I'd heard about his parties for years, but—probably because I was happily married and out of the "social circuit" of Hollywood's visiting macho bachelors—I was never invited. Big John often said that "it was a great party, too bad you weren't available to come!"

John Wayne's two sons went to those parties regularly and apparently enjoyed them. They wandered into the house when the Duke was showing me through and didn't hesitate to ask about Big John Hamilton in spite of their father's warning to "shut up."

The house was not ranch style but quite casual. The Duke paused at every bedroom to say who had been an overnight guest in his home, and most of them were politicians. Wayne was a rabid Republican and didn't hesitate to say, "I wouldn't have a lily-livered Democrat spend the night at my house!" Then he would dutifully take another swig of tequila.

It was a politically confusing age, with Nixon the center of attention. Wayne didn't mention Nixon by name but did insist that "if we didn't have

Conservative congressmen hard at work to protect our constitutional rights, the country would go to hell in a handbasket!"

He didn't have much to say about his fellow Hollywoodites although I remember Bruce Cabot's name cropping up a time or two. Cabot was a character actor who appeared in many Wayne westerns. Walter Brennan's name cropped up, too, and not always in a complimentary way. Although Wayne didn't say anything derogatory, he made it clear that he didn't count Walter Brennan among his best friends. It was the respectful thing to do because Brennan had died the previous year. Besides, he made only two movies with the Duke, to my knowledge.

Chill Wills's name came up, and Wayne didn't hesitate to call him a few names.

"Do you know what Chill did?" he asked.

"He took out ads and literally begged his fellow actors to vote for him as Best Supporting Actor for 'The Alamo.' He was trying to buy the award, and it wasn't for sale." (Chill Wills was nominated for "The Alamo," but Peter Ustinov won for "Spartacus" that year).

When I could get a word in edgewise, I asked John Wayne if he had a favorite role or character, and he just laughed.

"Hell, no. My favorite character is myself. I always play John Wayne in my movies. Since you're a movie critic, you should know that!"

He also referred to his western movies as "pop art" and his leading ladies as "that red-headed one" or "the blonde who knew how to play a sympathetic whore in 'Stagecoach'." It didn't take long to realize the blonde was Claire Trevor and the "red-headed one" was probably Maureen O'Hara, as she made several movies with the Duke.

"I didn't ask you about your politics, but if you're a Democrat, just keep your mouth shut," he said at one point. I took the hint and didn't say a word.

"What about golf? Do you play? Or do you like to sail boats?"

His questions were to the point and so were my answers. I told him that I was probably the most avid movie fan he's likely to meet ("Oh, but I've met a lot of them out here," he said) and I considered movie-going a solid participating sport. He laughed at that remark, then took another gulp of tequila and turned serious again. He was in the middle of reeling off a list of recent overnight guests when his white-jacketed servant came in with a tray of sweets. "Would the gent'man like dessert?" he asked. Wayne answered for both of us.

"Yes, we want some," he said.

It was a very satisfying trip, and "Brannigan" was more successful than the studio anticipated. They explained that they only have confidence in a John Wayne movie if he wears a cowboy hat, spurs, and chaps!

True to my word, I never called Big John Hamilton and told him anything about the trip. But he read my columns so I knew he would read about the dinner in John Wayne's home. One night when I drove into the Fox Theater parking lot, I saw a Cadillac swerve ahead of me and stop just inches away from the grill on my car. It was Big John Hamilton.

"Say, Bob, did the Duke ask about me when you saw him in Hollywood?"

"He didn't have to. I volunteered information about you. I told him you sent your regards!" That pacified the bombastic Big John and every time I saw him after that he would boast about the times he had with "my pal, John Wayne."

One time it even got a little ludicrous. It was 1978 when I was at a press screening of "Superman—the Movie" and an usher came to me and said I had an urgent phone call. The call was from Big John Hamilton, and the conversation went something like this:

"Bob, did you hear Chill Wills died?"

I answered that I hadn't.

"It just happened, and I'm packing my clothes now. They want me in Hollywood to plan Chill's funeral."

When I was weighing words to see what I could possibly say to Hamilton, he had an urgent question for me.

"Well, what are you going to do about it?"

"Do about what?"

"Aren't you going to write it in your column? I'm going to be in charge of Chill Wills' funeral."

If I had had my way at that moment I would have wished for John Wayne's presence. He would have known what to say to the bombastic, over-bearing Big John Hamilton, and I could just hear him doing it!

"What's wrong with you, you old fool," is probably what the Duke would have told Big John.

And he probably would have added, "Do you have enough class to just make the arrangements and keep your mouth shut about it?"

Most of us who grew up on John Wayne movies could always second-guess what the Duke might say. We always knew he would find a way of making his meaning clear and would know just what words to use for any and all occasions.

3.
THE INIMITABLE BARBRA STREISAND

BARBRA STREISAND ISN'T LOVABLE AND KNOWS IT. SHE THINKS SHE HAS distinction because of her flamboyant behavior so she puts on airs to show her power over situations. She also has an ego that would shatter glass, and she can shatter other people's egos with an intense look from fifty paces away, if she wants to.

But she has glamour—that indefinable quality that attracts people to her. We want to see her. We want to hear her sing and listen to her talk. Her talent dazzles everyone, even those who know she is very self-involved.

Her attitudes affect her peers in show business more than they affect outsiders in the press. Most of Hollywood's major stars and executives don't like to work with her or claim her as a friend. She's uptight as well as self-involved. That's why she doesn't make many movies.

To her credit, she can loosen up at the drop of a hat. Especially when she has her own money invested in a picture. It makes her aware of her effect on others, and that's a compliment, not an insult. Newspaper writers know this instinctively. Interviewers—and there aren't many press people outside of New York and Hollywood who are granted an interview with her—usually let her do all the talking. Whether we like it or not, she's going to answer the questions she wants asked. Even if she has to twist things around.

I've met her twice, and both times were memorable. Not for what she said as much as for the way she said it. She revealed her attitude with body language and voice inflections so I learned more about her from our interview than from any of the publicity comments attributed to her.

Our first meeting was in 1975 when she was working on the remake of "A Star Is Born" for her own company, Barwood Productions. Her live-in boyfriend, Jon Peters, was credited as producer and both of them wanted it released in 1976 as one of the Hollywood events for the Bicentennial.

When it was Streisand's turn to be interviewed, she put Peters on the back burner by proudly telling one and all that she was not only the film's star but also its producer. What's more, she was the songwriter for the rock songs in this version of the famous story. (At the Oscar ceremony she won an Oscar for cowriting the song "Evergreen" with lyricist Paul Williams.)

But let's back up to the events leading to the interview. Everything was carefully planned because Barbra Streisand understands the value of prerelease interviews to start word-of-mouth interest. She realized she had to shed her cold, calculating image long enough to get the press to praise her efforts. It was her idea to invite a group of newspaper writers to Tempe, Arizona, to watch a scene being filmed and have an informal talk with her and select cast members.

She was also astute enough to whet our appetites with an action scene. Watching her act would be invading her idea of privacy, so she allowed us to witness an action scene that did not involve her.

In that scene, Kris Kristofferson rode his motorcycle off the stage during a concert being held in the crowded stadium. We saw a stuntman take his place for the action crash. We also saw Kristofferson pose for close-ups before and after the scene. You could say it was a crash course in movie-making for Streisand's hand-picked audience.

She also saved payroll money by inviting the press people to be in the stadium as part of the crowd. We were to sit in the stadium with the extras hired for that day, and all of us would watch Kristofferson's motorcycle run off the stage. When you see the scene, you'll notice that the camera doesn't dwell on the crash. Instead, it takes a long shot of the crowded stadium, and I was one of those extras in the top row. You can't blink, though, or you'll miss my "debut." All eight of us at the junket were so excited we didn't mind doing the scene without pay.

Afterwards, representatives from Warner Brothers (distributors of the film) reminded us that we were now part of an historic picture. Streisand's "A Star Is Born" was actually the fourth version of the story. The first was called "What Price Hollywood?" with Constance Bennett and was filmed in 1932. The second was the Janet Gaynor-Fredric March version called "A Star Is Born" (1937). The third was the first musical version, and it used the "Star Is Born" title. It starred Judy Garland (1954). Streisand's 1975 version changed the musical format. She wanted to "update" the picture with a rock score.

After our "historic" scene, we gathered around a portable table on the stadium grounds for interviews. There was plenty of wine and some finger sandwiches to help us pass the time, and I took the most strategic seat at the table—right next to the chair reserved for the interviewee. It had to be, because it was the only seat in the shade.

Streisand was not the first interviewee. She positioned herself last so she could have the last word. The first to be interviewed was her leading man, Kris Kristofferson, and he came in with a half-filled glass of wine in his hand. It was probably the first of several since he was slurring words.

"I'm in this movie and glad of it even if I was second choice. Barbra made no bones about the fact that she wanted Elvis to be her leading man. She met with him, but Elvis is no dummy. He figured Barbra just wanted someone to front for her. The movie is definitely a 'Barbra Streisand Show'."

He drank the rest of the wine and signaled the waiter for another. It was obvious that he was angry about having been second choice and probably felt he was being taken advantage of.

The next interviewee was Jon Peters, Barbra's boyfriend. He was intense. A fiery ambition motivated him, and it showed in his eyes. He started by praising Barbra to the hilt. He knew it was her movie—not his—and he took the easy way out. By praising Streisand, he reflected gentlemanly good taste. He also showed he had a sense of humor about himself.

"This is the first movie I've worked on, but I feel like a seasoned producer," he said, reaffirming his position by steadfastly refusing the wine offered him. It made all of us perk up our ears. Here was a producer who intended to keep his wits about him.

"I have many friends in the business, and I've kept up with the business over the years. I have several more movies on my drawing board now."

The next year he would produce "The Eyes of Laura Mars" with Faye Dunaway. He also had "The Main Event" (another Barbra Streisand movie) ready to start filming.

From 1982 to 1989, Peters and his friend, Peter Guber, ran Columbia Pictures, bringing such modern-day classics as "Missing" and "Flash Dance" to the screen. Peters would stay in the movie business throughout the 1980s and into the 1990s, working on such interesting failures as "Bonfire of the Vanities" and "Tango and Cash." He also had interesting successes, most notably "The Color Purple" and "Batman." "A Star Is Born" came somewhere in between. It was successful with Streisand fans but paled in comparison with the earlier Judy Garland version.

When he parted company with Streisand, he got out of the spotlight in order to keep his private life private. For her part, she never mentions him. At least, not to the press.

Her life now revolves around her husband, James Brolin. They had a very successful wedding event in the 1990s (staged by Streisand herself) and a guest list that included President and Mrs. Bill Clinton. It was publicized in all the papers and magazines at that time, but—if you noticed—no interviews with the bride were in those publications.

The next interview for "A Star Is Born" was Director Frank Pierson, and he didn't gulp down a glass of wine before we asked a question. Like Kris Kristofferson and Jon Peters, he knew he was not picked for his skills but for his attitude. He was wise enough to let Streisand call the shots and accept the idea that he was a director in name only. He didn't say that, but it was obvious by the way he described the way "Barbra wanted to set up the scene" and the reasons why "Barbra wanted to have a bathtub love scene with Kris Kristofferson."

Pierson had earned an Oscar for cowriting "Dog Day Afternoon" the year before, so he had good credentials. He was quick to tell us that "A Star Is Born" was the first movie to list him as the official director. It was apparent to us that he was involved in the movie as a shield for Barbra Streisand, just as Jon Peters was.

True to form, Streisand was the last person to be interviewed, and she acted as if she knew she was the "grand finale." She was in the spotlight, and Kristofferson, Peters, and Pierson had warmed up the audience for her.

She literally glittered with glamour, and not only because she didn't have the fizzy hairdo she wears in the picture. Barbra Streisand was and is a unique show business personality, and we accepted her at face value until her ego got in the way.

She got off on the wrong foot by having Leo Wilder, head of Warner Brothers Press Relations at the time, prepare us for her entrance with a list of questions she wanted us to ask. Each was about how important this picture was to her career.

To Wilder's surprise, we told him we wouldn't interview her on those terms. We wanted to ask our own questions. Wilder begrudgingly backed off with a parting shot to remind us that Warner Brothers was "happy to pay your way to Arizona to meet and talk to Barbra Streisand." Our response was complete silence.

Of course, he knew Streisand would be smart enough to twist every question around so that she could use the words and phrases she had already selected to "sell" her picture. She also had enough pride not to give any mass interviews after that. At least, not for several years.

Meanwhile, she singled me out of the group, but not because I didn't greet her with the comments Wilder asked us to use. She stared me down coldly while smiling outwardly when I spilled a glass of wine onto her lap.

It was an accident and an embarrassing one. It happened when another reporter (Shirley Eder from a Detroit newspaper) pulled the empty chair away from my side of the table before I could stop her. She said, "Here, Barbra, sit next to me," and Barbra complied.

The only thing I could do was move my tape recorder across the table to get all her comments. In so doing, I spilled that fateful glass of wine.

Streisand was obviously angry but smart enough not to show it. She said, "What are you trying to do? Make a lasting impression on my pantsuit?" She laughed, but the coldness in her eyes reflected her true feelings.

I met her again in 1991 when she starred in and directed "Prince of Tides." She was still every inch a prima donna and still played it to the hilt. It was her first group interview since 1975, and she took part in it by rotating tables of interviewers gathered from major cities across the country.

Bob Polunsky's Flicker Footnotes

Others in the cast (Nick Nolte, Blythe Danner, Kate Nelligan, Streisand's son Jason Gould, plus screenwriter and original author Pat Conroy) also rotated tables so all of us got interviews at the same time.

Streisand would pause before answering a question to blow a kiss to Jason. He played her son in the film, and it was his only major film appearance despite his mother's attempt to build him up to press and public.

Jason's father, Elliott Gould, was Streisand's first husband when he was a bigger star than she was. He had the lead in the Broadway musical "I Can Get It for You Wholesale." Streisand had only one musical number in the show ("Miss Marmelstein"). They met and were married during the run of that show. Then along came "Funny Girl" and Streisand was suddenly a bigger star than her husband. They separated and finally divorced in a real-life version of the plot of "A Star Is Born."

Nobody at the press junket cared much for Jason. He answered our questions as if he had been carefully rehearsed, and his behavior was very affected. His main comments were about his mother as he praised her ability as the director (an official designation this time) as well as the star.

Although she didn't get anyone to give us prearranged questions this time, Streisand squeezed in every comment she could to make herself look important. She told us she took over "Prince of Tides" when "no one else knew how to condense the massive novel into a workable movie." She also told us that her friend, Robert Redford (her costar in "The Way We Were" in 1973) had originally optioned the book but couldn't get it together. She implied he recommended her to make the movie. Whether he did or not is irrelevant. What was important was that Streisand used Redford's name and reputation to put herself in the spotlight.

Pat Conroy's novel is long and involved, but she used only part of it—the part about the character's romance with the story's hero (Nick Nolte). Streisand played his psychiatrist, who counseled him about his emotional problems even though she had emotional problems of her own. Her screen husband (Jeroen Krabbe) was an egomaniac obsessed with his own importance as an orchestra conductor. He put his career above his family's welfare. Nolte's character helped her resolve her emotional problems so he was just as much of a doctor for her as she was for him. He was exceptionally good (and he credited Streisand's direction), and Streisand assured us he was a surefire bet for an Oscar nomination. She also predicted nominations for most of the cast.

Actually, she wasn't too far off. "Prince of Tides" was nominated for Best Picture, Nick Nolte for Best Actor, Kate Nelligan for Best Supporting Actress, and Pat Conroy for adapting his novel to the screen. None of them won. Neither Barbra Streisand nor her son, Jason, was nominated.

Her comment was meant to put thoughts in the back of our heads. If we talked up the movie and praised her ability, she just might get nominated for

Best Director. It would have been a prestigious award if she were the first woman accorded an Oscar for directing a movie. Then—and now, too—women rarely got to direct a major film.

She was manipulating the press to her own advantage, but not as obviously as she did for "A Star Is Born" fifteen years earlier. I doubt if she remembered much about that interview session nor the wine incident. Her pantsuit with the wine stain was probably thrown out immediately.

I hadn't forgotten it nor was I prepared for another confrontation, but we had one after the interviews for "Prince of Tides." It was when I asked for her autograph and handed her two different still pictures to sign. One would be for me and the other would be for a coworker.

She hesitated. Giving autographs was not the sort of thing a star of Barbra Streisand's stature did. It was a little too common, but she reluctantly took one of the stills and smiled condescendingly as she said, "All you can have is one."

4.
BLONDE SEX SYMBOL SMACKS POLUNSKY!
(AND IT MADE THE PAPERS!)

I REMEMBER THE HEADLINE AS IF IT WERE YESTERDAY. BLONDE SEX SYMBOL SMACKS POLUNSKY! Five words encased in a balloon that was in the banner across the top of the newspaper's front page.

The words sounded as if a very sexy blonde had slapped me, but if you turned to the page with the story it was just an innocent "smack"—a kiss on the cheek—from blonde sex symbol Ann Jillian. It was my first story in the San Antonio Express-News after I resigned from the Light.

I spent sixteen years at the Light, and the people were good to me. But there were problems with various editors, so I couldn't resist an offer from the rival paper that promised me I would be in control of my interview material. They would pay me a flat fee that was five times as much money as I was being paid at the Light. Bert Wise, the managing editor, also promised that I would be the main attraction on the movie pages. I had a guarantee of a Sunday column and as many movie reviews as I wanted to write during the week. All for a flat fee that was more than ample.

The Light paid me by the piece, and it was only for the pieces they printed. Granted, they printed most of what I wrote as long as I didn't write more than two reviews per week. All interview pages had to be approved in advance. Besides, they had just hired a new overseer for the entertainment section. He was coming to town fresh from a New York City job where he had "first refusal" on all junket invitations and "first call" for all the "important" reviews and interviews. With those kind of changes on the horizon, I didn't hesitate to accept the Express-News offer of a job that ended—ironically—when the Hearst Corporation, owners of the Light, bought the Express-News years down the line. For now, I had the terrific introduction of being "smacked" by that "blonde sex symbol."

Ann Jillian was a movie star with ties to San Antonio. She was a breast cancer victim and came to San Antonio for help and advice. She got advice from my good friend, Bob Stewart, the Light's TV critic at the time. Bob's wife, Martha, was also afflicted with breast cancer. She and Ann Jillian became fast friends and went through cancer surgery together. Bob and

Ann's husband wrote an inspirational book about their surgery and recovery, and it was well received all over the country.

Now that the surgery was over, Ann was ready to go back to the movie business, where she had started as "Little Bo Peep" in a big-screen version of "Babes in Toyland." She also played Baby Jane to Natalie Wood's Gypsy Rose Lee in the movie version of "Gypsy." When cancer reared its ugly head, Ann disappeared from the screen. When she returned to show business, it was mostly in a string of not-too-successful TV series. Sometimes she had a supporting role (as in early "Hazel" episodes) and one time she played the lead. It was in "Jennifer Slept Here," a sitcom about a movie sex symbol whose ghost haunted her previous home. She wasn't a scary kind of ghost. She was the kind who helped the new owners of her house solve their problems. The series lasted only a year, but Ann—as usual—was memorable.

An invitation to interview Michael Keaton and Teri Garr at a "Mr. Mom" junket was a dream come true, as I heard what glib interviewees they were from friends on both the East and West coasts.

The junket sounded even better when I found out Ann Jillian would be there. I had seen her on TV and was familiar with her early movie career. I also heard a lot about her from Bob Stewart. My only disappointment was that she wore a red wig in the movie, and I had always been a sucker for blonde beauties. But the interview itself couldn't have been better.

"I hadn't made a movie since 'Gypsy,' and that was over twenty years ago," she said, when I asked why she wanted to play a home-wrecker.

"When I read the script of 'Mr. Mom,' I realized the villainess was full of personality. That's the kind of character I really want to play. Not many movie villainesses are as clever, and I liked the idea of thumbing my nose at movie villainy. I took the job even though it meant I had to hide my hair!"

She also took it in order to be a good foil for Teri Garr and Michael Keaton. They played the married couple that was threatened by Ann's character, mainly because the husband (Michael Keaton) was at home all the time and readily available. He played chief cook and bottle-washer at home after losing his job. His wife still had a good job, so he let her be the breadwinner. This meant he was on hand to hear all of the neighbors' problems. In time, he was one of those family problems, and that's where Ann Jillian came in.

"I also liked the idea of making a family movie with some wholesome characters because it's such a rare opportunity these days," Ann said.

"The movie is about a marriage that almost falls apart, but it's handled without profanity or raw sex. Those are the main things I object to in today's 'family' movies. They don't belong on the screen, just in the audience's imaginations."

Ann also talked about her stage career when she was performing with Mickey Rooney and Ann Miller in the original cast of "Sugar Babies." She called it a unique experience that proved to be "very rewarding."

"The excitement and spontaneity of the stage is rewarding because of the edge it gives to the performer," she said.

"You have to perform for a different audience every night, and no two audiences are the same so no two performances are the same. It's the kind of excitement you can't get anywhere else in show business, with the possible exception of a 'live' TV show."

"What about film?"

"By its very nature, film captures an emotion forever. It's always going to be there for audiences to respond to so it gives an actress a sense of immortality."

"What about the role of Mae West you did on TV? You recreated some famous scenes and comments by Mae West, but you did it in your own voice and with your own personality."

"It felt like I was a resurrected Mae West so I was immortalizing her in my own way. It was still with her words. The only changes were my inflection and my version of her personality. Did you know I was in the running for a big-screen movie biography of Mae West?"

I admitted I didn't know there was going to be one.

"There won't be, now that the TV version clicked. But at one time, two different movies about Mae West were being considered. I feel fortunate to be in the TV version because of the Emmy nomination I received. The idea of being in the same league as Ingrid Bergman [an Emmy winner for her impersonation of Golda Meir that year] was thrilling. I couldn't help but hope that some of Ingrid's glitz and glamour—and acting ability—rubbed off on me."

Ann was very open with the facts of her life and career. She is such a down-to-earth human being that it was easy to talk to her without notes. She gave me a good interview and made it memorable because she gave me a big kiss on the cheek on camera. It left a big red imprint on my check, and I told her I would never wash it off. But I was challenged by my next interview.

"Hey, you've got a big red lipstick print on your check," Michael Keaton said when we were introduced.

"I know, and it's going to stay there," I said.

"I don't want anyone to think I put it there," Keaton then said.

"No danger about that, Mr. Keaton. Everyone knows I don't let men kiss me."

The TV cameramen laughed heartily and Michael Keaton looked a little surprised. I think he was a little jealous. Not of Ann Jillian's kiss but of my response to him. He apparently planned his joke to be at my expense. It turned out to be just the opposite.

It was six years before I interviewed Michael Keaton again, and it was for "Batman," a much bigger and more successful movie than "Mr. Mom." But he acted pretty much the same as he had at the "Mr. Mom" junket, with self-centered jokes that begged for a laugh or, at the very least, a good smirk.

Keaton liked laughing at himself and enjoyed it even better when people laughed at the "digs" he made at and about himself. He rarely let anyone else's joke get a better laugh. It was a self-defense technique to garner all the attention.

It sounded too childish for the personable Mr. Keaton, but "Mr. Mom" proved my point. He played the Nice Guy who takes care of the kids, makes the beds, washes the dishes, and fixes dinner. Each episode in the film was designed to get laughs, and it worked to a large degree. But the biggest laughed turned out to be on Michael Keaton when he was a helpless husband trying to defend himself from the womanly wiles of an aggressive woman. In other words, this kind of situation could lead to heavy-breathing melodrama. In "Mr. Mom" it led to a scene with Ann Jillian as an aggressive man-chaser getting her comeuppance. It also meant Ann Jillian successfully competed with Michael Keaton, the comedian, because she got all the laughs. All it took was a kiss to make him take a back seat to the action.

I understood her tactics completely. She did the same to me with a kiss during our interview.

5.
JANE WITHERS LASSOED A CAREER

SOME OF THE OLD-TIMERS WERE MY BEST INTERVIEWS. ESPECIALLY WOMEN, because they are easier to read. Women are masters of inflection even though they often disguise the meaning behind their words. They can be frustrating, but they can also be fun. Especially if all this put-on stuff doesn't interfere with a budding friendship. Being a friend to a celebrity is usually a short-order affair, but there's usually a sense of trust that can't be overlooked.

It was apparent when I tried to get hold of Jane Withers, the former child star who hadn't made a movie in over thirty years.

It was in February of 1999, just a few months before the fiftieth reunion of my high school class, and I was asked to be in charge of the committee. Working on a reunion was fun because we got to relive our youth. That's what gave me the idea to court an old-time movie star and make her part of the festivities. Since I wasn't sure how things would work out, I kept my plan a secret, telling the committee only that I wanted to make the most of my ties with Hollywood to make our fiftieth reunion the best ever. They didn't interfere. No one else in the committee had ties to Hollywood, and they left it in my hands. Their trust made me doubly careful. I wanted to make sure this plan worked.

Jane Withers was considered "one of us." Every Jefferson student felt that way, at least from 1940 on. Jane—we all felt we were on a first-name basis with her—came to San Antonio at the age of thirteen to make a movie at Thomas Jefferson High School. It was called "High School," and there were no surprises in it except for the fact that Jane Withers was playing her first teenage role. She played a Lasso, a member of the school's well-known drill team. Unlike typical Lassoes (by reputation anyway), she was a mischief-maker and a troublemaker, who redeemed herself in the end. In most of her pictures she either got a spanking or a good talking-to, leading to a happy ending and an about-face for the Withers personality.

I intended to invite her as our guest of honor strictly because she had once played a Lasso, filmed it at our high school, and was a major celebrity to all of us. No one else from Hollywood had made a movie at our high school.

I called Bob Easton, a dialect coach in Hollywood and a one-time classmate. He had attended Thomas Jefferson High School from 1947 to 1949 after making a name for himself as one of the national "Quiz Kids" in Chicago. He and I were friends then, and I renewed that relationship when I asked him to cohost a Movie Cruise with me during the 1980s. He agreed out of respect for our friendship, because no money changed hands, and I was grateful that he was so agreeable.

I asked Bob to come to the reunion, and he said he would try. I also asked if he knew Jane Withers, and he said he did. I explained that I wanted her to be our Guest of Honor since she had once made a movie at our school.

"You don't have to tell me that," he said. "But you're barking up the wrong tree. Jane has nothing to do with Hollywood stuff any more. She's active in church work, designs her own clothes, and pretty much stays to herself. She feels disappointed with her old career because none of her movies are on cable or video, and all of Shirley Temple's movies are. They were contemporaries, you know. She probably won't even talk to you."

"I still want to try. Have her call me or get her to give you her number. I won't be satisfied until I've talked to her."

To make a long story short, he called me back with her phone number and another warning. "She says she's not interested but is willing to talk to you." I then made the call.

Jane Withers answered the phone herself and was formal but pleasant. "Why do you want me there? I haven't been to San Antonio for 60 years. Nobody in your class would remember me."

"Oh, yes, they would. We all do, because you're one of us. You are the only Hollywood star who ever made a movie at our school and you played a Lasso. That's big-time stuff to Jefferson High students no matter what year it happened."

She was silent for a minute, then said, "Well, I'm flattered. When is this shindig and what do you want me to do."

The plan was under way. I explained the entire weekend and said all expenses would be paid, of course.

"First-class air fare?"

"Yes."

"Good. Traveling coach is too cramped, don't you think? Of course, I'm older than you. I'm seventy-three. How old are you?"

Things were going better than I thought. She was downright friendly. I decided to play the "Treat the has-been like a star" routine and started talking about her old movies, but she interrupted me.

"I know you want to be nice, but this is ridiculous. If you remember any of my old movies, you've got too much time on your hands. They don't make movies like that any more, and I'm not fooling myself about my career. I made forty-seven movies and had a helluva good time, but all that is over. I have better things to do with my time than live in the past."

This gal was on the ball. She's going to be a great guest of honor, and fit right in with the rest of us.

But she was more of a prima donna the next time I called. She asked what she was going to have for dinner.

"I keep regular hours, and my dinnertime in Los Angeles is two hours ahead of anyone in San Antonio so I'll be hungry by the time we land. Does this hotel you're putting me in have all-night room service?"

Jane was trying to be subtle. She wanted to know if it was a first-class hotel, since they are about the only hotels with twenty-four-hour-service. She was just too nice to come out and ask if it was a luxury hotel or not.

"We think too much of your privacy to put you on display at a major downtown hotel," I told her. "It would be more private and more comfortable if we just put you up at a small residential hotel with all the comforts of a major hotel but at a lower rate. That's to our benefit, of course, but we're not short-changing you. They have a restaurant, but if it's closed by the time you register, I'll take you to a nice place, I promise."

She seemed satisfied, and I mopped my brow. Jane Withers was going to keep me on my toes, and she would be tougher than Madonna. My interview with Madonna only lasted about twenty minutes. Interviewing Jane Withers was going to take a full weekend.

True to my word, I took her to the Crystal Baking Company, a steak house on Loop 410 with a great reputation, thanks mostly to the charm of its owner, Tom Tasos. Tom serves great steaks with all the trimmings. I expected that, but I really wanted to take advantage of his charm with the women. I asked him to make a fuss over her, and he was glad to do it.

When he met her, he kissed her hand and greeted her as if she were the biggest star in Hollywood. Jane seemed completely taken by him. At least, I thought so until she winked at me. It was a sign she knew what I was doing and appreciated it.

Our reunion lasted from Friday night to Sunday night, but Jane didn't come to town until Saturday so she was with us only for the last two days. Everyone was not only surprised but genuinely shocked when they saw her. She looked just as she had in the movies, with nary a wrinkle showing. Her hair was solid black—not a strand of gray—and she had abandoned the hair bob of her youth for an upswept hairdo. She looked great! She was also very energetic, laughing a lot and asking all kinds of questions about the Lassoes, San Antonio, and Jefferson High. She didn't wait for people to ask her questions. She jumped right into conversations as if she had known everyone at the Reunion for a lifetime.

"Hollywood is a small town and a great one, I think," she said. "I've always had plenty of friends and plenty of things to do there. It's my home town now, although I was born in Atlanta and go back there every now and then to see old friends.

"I have lunch every few weeks in Hollywood with actresses from 'my day' and that corresponds to your high school days. One of my best lunch companions is Joan Brodel. Oops. I forgot. You know her by her screen name of Joan Leslie. She was Jimmy Cagney's wife in 'Yankee Doodle Dandy' and Gary Cooper's wife in 'Sergeant York.' Joan and I never made a movie together, but we've been friends for years. She appreciates church work just like I do. The only difference is she's a Catholic, and I'm a Presbyterian. I'll bet Catholics and Presbyterians make equally good Lassoes, don't they?"

Like a real pro, Jane "involved" her audience. She may not make movies any more, but she knew how to hold an audience's interest.

Every now and then someone asked her about her Jeff High movie, "High School."

"I thought you'd never ask," she answered with a laugh. "I brought a couple of copies of the movie with me. I thought you might like to see what Jeff High looked like in the 1940s. I also hoped you'd like to see what I looked like then. I brought two copies on tape so you can put them at opposite ends of the dance floor if you want to."

We certainly did want to but they caused a traffic jam on the dance floor, so we moved the tapes to a separate room at the ranch where we had our Saturday night dinner and dance.

On Sunday Jane added a different kind of spice to the reunion. She invited her son, Bill Moss, Jr, to come in from the Rio Grande Valley where he lives. She didn't ask me if it was okay. She just assumed it would be.

"I thought your Jeff high pals would like to be with someone a little younger," she explained. Bill—like his mother—was energetic and cheerful. He also ate enough barbecue to be a high school student.

Jane Withers made an indelible impression on students who knew her only as a child star with Shirley Temple (they made one movie together) and a teenager from "High School." Being with her was an adventure, and she kept it interesting by keeping us guessing. She was completely natural so I can't say she was just being an actress. But I can say she gave a great performance and wrapped it all up with a quotable farewell. When the weekend was over, she leaned over and said, "I want you to know you paid me a great compliment." Thinking she meant she appreciated being invited, I assured her the pleasure was really ours.

"No, you don't understand," she said without pausing for breath. "I don't mean the invitation to come to San Antonio. I mean what you said on the phone that first time. Do you remember telling me I was one of you? You put me in the same category as all Jefferson High students at the reunion, and it made me feel like a teenager again."

6.
OLIVIA, 2; JOAN, 1

LIKE MOST MOVIE BUFFS, I HAD HEARD ABOUT THE FEUD BETWEEN SISTERS Olivia DeHavilland and Joan Fontaine. They never made a movie together. All their bickering took place behind the scenes, not in front of the cameras.

There was a plan to costar them in "Devotion," the story of the Bronte sisters. Olivia was to play Charlotte, the strong one and author of "Jane Eyre." Joan was slated for Emily, the consistently mixed-up one and author of "Wuthering Heights." But the sisters did not get along, so they refused to make the picture together. The movie was still made in 1943, with Ida Lupino replacing Joan, but it was shelved until 1946 because Warner Brothers wanted to use their movies for morale-builders as long as World War II was going on and "Devotion" was a downer.

Olivia was a two-time Oscar winner. Joan earned just one, but she received her Oscar first. Although neither sister said so, their enmity was supposed to stem from the time Joan won her Oscar in 1941.

There were photographs in the newspapers indicating the closeness of the sisters in the early 1940s. They supported each other when Olivia was nominated for "Gone with the Wind" only to lose to Hattie McDaniel, whose portrayal of Mammy was one of the best performances in the show.

There were more photographs of the sisters together the next year when Joan was nominated for "Rebecca," but lost to Ginger Rogers (a winner for "Kitty Foyle.") The next year was a tricky one. Joan was up for "Suspicion" and Olivia for "Hold Back the Dawn." The sisters were competing against each other, and Joan won. Or so Olivia apparently said. She spurned her sister at the Oscar ceremonies and they've had an open feud going ever since.

In the meantime Olivia won an Oscar for "To Each His Own" (1946) and "The Heiress" (1949). She also moved to Paris and came back only for special occasions. One time it was to play a featured role in "Airport 77." This was the third in the "Airport" series and major junkets were rarely held for sequels. Especially sequels that basically repeated the plot of the original film.

That was probably the reason why Universal Pictures decided on a different kind of junket. Reporters were invited to the location shooting while filming was in progress. It was the same thing Warner Brothers had done with "A Star Is Born" the previous year.

They picked a day when several name stars were working. James Stewart, Jack Lemmon, and Lee Grant were working on the day scheduled. So was Olivia DeHavilland.

It was a rough day of filming, and the stars showed it. James Stewart came to the little conference room improvised on the barren land in the desert around Los Angeles. Only a few wild-growing shrubs were showing. As usual, Stewart was nonplussed. He would scratch his raggedy beard and answer with little more than a "yup" or a "nope."

"This isn't an Oscar-winning movie," Stewart said. He had won an Oscar for "The Philadelphia Story" in 1940.

"It's made to capitalize on the 'Airport' movies, and those movies have lots of fans. They call them program pictures because they're made to fulfill a specific need. They need these kinds of pictures as much as I—and probably you—needed a western to round out a program when we were kids. There's not much to the plot. It just ties loose ends together with enough action to fill out the time."

Jack Lemmon—who won his first Oscar for "Mr. Roberts" in 1955 and was to win another Oscar for "Save the Tiger" in 1973—was more enthusiastic but didn't say a lot more.

"Working on a picture like this is as good as watching them at a movie theater. You get involved in the excitement, the mystery—whatever's at hand. Working on one is like taking a vacation from work. It's physically exhausting. But it's also lots of fun."

Later that day I saw Jack Lemmon do a scene. He wore an all-rubber suit when he had to be immersed in water for the scene. The junket reporters gathered on the sidelines to watch Jack and the others get out of the water. I managed to be right in the center and was close to the water.

When the scene was over, Jack stepped out and walked to the sidelines laughing. "Yep, like I said. It was lots of fun!"

When we had a break, I walked in and out of the rows of portable dressing rooms, hoping to find someone for an impromptu interview. I didn't find one, but one of the stars found me. It was Lee Grant, Oscar winner for Best Supporting Actress for the recently released "Shampoo."

She said, "Hello. Are you lost?"

I assured her I wasn't lost, just looking for celebrities. She puffed on her cigarette, then asked, "What's your name?" When I told her, she said she had a friend by that name and asked if I were any relation to him.

"His name is Abe Polonsky. He's a writer. He wrote 'Body and Soul' and 'Tell Them Willie Boy Is Here.' He writes good screenplays."

I agreed, saying I wished I were related to him. Even getting to meet him would be an honor.

"Maybe some day you will. What do you think of the setup for 'Airport 77'? Does it look good to you?"

"With a cast like this, it can't miss."

The cast was good but I still had not met my heroine, Olivia DeHavilland. I went back to our office, which was set up in a tent, and asked about her. The publicity agent said she was working on a scene in which she, like Jack Lemmon, gets dunked.

"Olivia won't come out till she gets her hair dry, I'm sure," the agent said. "But I'll check on her."

Just a very few minutes had passed when the agent came back with Olivia DeHavilland dressed in a pink bathrobe with a towel wrapped around her head, turban style.

Introductions were made; then we took our seats in front of a TV camera, and I sat there wide-eyed. The camera was not yet turned on when Olivia asked if something was the matter.

"No. It's just that it's every red-blooded American boy's dream to meet Maid Marian, and I feel lucky to have done so."

She laughed. "I was Maid Marian forty-odd years ago when we made a version of 'Robin Hood.' I think I've aged a bit since then. But I still love that version of the story. Errol Flynn was positively wonderful."

She had a way of taking the spotlight away from herself while basking in its glow.

"You made several films with him. I take it he was your favorite costar?"

"Let's say he was one of them. Errol was dashing and young and handsome. Every girl my age admired him. You might say we all fell in love with him a little. Actresses do that, you know, and we generally do it with our leading men.

"Take Jack Lemmon, for example. He's my costar in 'Airport 77' and he's such a gentleman, and such a witty person, that I've fallen for him. At least a little bit. I also feel a little bit in love with Joseph Cotten (who was in the picture but wasn't at the junket). I've felt that way about him since we made 'Hush...Hush...Sweet Charlotte' together. And James Stewart. Who wouldn't fall in love with Jimmy. He's a delightful person. We dated each other for awhile when we were in our teens and early twenties."

Olivia also talked about the need for pictures like "Airport 77" ("It's no 'Gone with the Wind,' but how many pictures are?")

Like Jimmy Stewart and Jack Lemmon before her, she said the movie fulfilled the need for family pictures to fill out the slots for program pictures. Generally speaking, though, "Airport 77" was probably too expensive to be just "a program picture." The list of cast members made it a quality picture guaranteed first-run showings in first-run theaters.

"I understand you've spent a lot of time in my home town of San Antonio," I said.

"Oh, yes, and I love it. I have some dear friends who live there, and I have a place by Medina Lake. My children go to school in Austin."

Olivia gushed a bit, but that was to be expected. She's been gushing her lines ever since she played the gushy Melanie in "Gone with the Wind" (and was nominated for an Oscar for it).

I asked her about "Gone with the Wind."

"Do I resent Hattie McDaniel for winning the Oscar instead of me?" she asked. "Of course not! Hattie's winning the Oscar put an entirely new perspective on the film. No one can say it was proslavery, and it showed how well the O'Hara family and the Wilkes family treated their slaves. Hattie symbolized all the good things about the era…all the things she did in the movie to help Scarlett, Suellen, and Careen [Vivien Leigh, Evelyn Keyes, and Ann Rutherford in the film]. She was also a model of godliness to the rest of the characters in that wonderful story. I felt honored to be nominated in the same classification as she was!"

If any of the publicity about Olivia and the "Gone with the Wind" Oscar ceremony is to be believed, she did resent the situation. But it was only because she wanted to upstage her sister, Joan Fontaine, and win an Oscar first.

A few years later I met Joan Fontaine when she came to San Antonio to play the lead in "Wait Until Dark" at the Fiesta Dinner Playhouse. Appearing in dinner theater in San Antonio meant actors and actresses were either on the way up or on the way down. Joan's career had fizzled. She was no longer in demand for strong women's roles and she didn't like the "B" pictures she was offered. I knew enough to steer clear of that topic, but I still wanted to know how Joan Fontaine felt about it.

She let me know with her body language. She sat curled up in a big chair, pointing a well-manicured hand at me when I asked her questions.

"I don't make movies for my livelihood any more," she said.

"I make them when I like the part, and it doesn't matter if it's the lead or a supporting role. I guess the last 'important' picture I made was 'Serenade' opposite Mario Lanza. I played his mistress, only I held the purse strings, and that was in 1956. Before that Ida Lupino asked me to play an important role in her production of 'The Bigamist.' It was an important picture because it showed how divorces affect all parties involved. It was considered a low-budget film, but it had a strong story."

She only mentioned her sister Olivia once, and it was in passing.

"My sister managed to reach that professional tier of actors and actresses who stay popular no matter what. I never made it, but I've had a good time with my career and intend to keep plugging away."

Joan Fontaine's career had a beginning, middle, and end, and she was approaching the end when only low-budget movies were offered to her. In the beginning of her career she played the sole romantic character in "Gunga Din" and played Sam Houston's bitchy first wife in "Man of Conquest." In the middle of her career she was in such big-time pictures as "Rebecca" and "The Constant Nymph" (which she calls her favorite). The third and final phase is a career in low-budget films coupled with stage tours like the one she did when she played a blind girl in "Wait Until Dark" at San Antonio's Fiesta Dinner Playhouse.

Unlike her sister, Joan Fontaine doesn't attract a crowd every time she steps out. One reason is because she rarely smiles, and, when she does, her mouth looks crooked.

It's a shame that Olivia and Joan don't get along. Charlotte and Emily Bronte apparently had a love/hate relationship similar to the DeHavilland/Fontaine feud. It didn't come across in the movie, "Devotion," but—if Fontaine had played Emily to DeHavilland's Charlotte—the fur would certainly have flown. Just look at the way they are accepted today: Joan Fontaine is a one-time Oscar winner appearing as the second lead in low-budget productions. Two-time Oscar winner Olivia DeHavilland spends most of her time in France but comes back every so often to be in a picture. Chances are she'll have the lead in it, but even if she doesn't, her presence alone makes the movie more appealing. You can tell by the size of the crowd following her. Joan Fontaine attracted a medium-sized crowd for her performance in the Fiesta Playhouse production of "Wait Until Dark." Sure, she got publicity in the local media, but it was as lukewarm as the applause when she made her entrance.

Olivia DeHavilland attracted a bigger crowd just for making a movie. Reporters from all over the country watched her dunk her head in the water for a minor scene in a minor movie, "Airport 77." What's more important is that her makeshift audience applauded her.

7.
PIA'S POLACK

PIA ZADORA CALLED ME HER "LITTLE POLACK!"

We met in 1983 while she was working on "Lonely Lady," the movie that was supposed to kick off her "leading lady" career. Before that she made "Santa Claus Conquers the Martians" (1964) and the soft-porn "Butterfly" (1981). "Lonely Lady" was based on a trashy Harold Robbins novel, and nobody wrote better trash than Robbins.

Pia's agent phoned to tell me she was available for interviews for her forthcoming film on a limited basis, and only in person. Pia did not like phoners. She was filming in Houston and wanted me to visit the set.

I explained that Houston was two hundred miles away from San Antonio. Contrary to popular thought, all Texas towns don't border one another, and I couldn't take off for Houston to do an interview for a movie not yet in release.

"Well, Pia has to fly to Dallas so we could fly you to Houston and you could board a plane with her and talk to her on the way to Dallas," the agent said. "Don't worry. We'll fly you back home well ahead of your deadline."

I thanked her but told her I was going to a junket in a couple of days so I couldn't take advantage of her offer. Perhaps she could let me interview Pia when the picture was ready for release. She said she would try.

She called back in less than five minutes to ask where the junket was, and who would I be talking to? She was polite but obviously curious.

"Actually, I'm going to two junkets on the same weekend. One in Los Angeles and one in New York City," I told her.

"Where will you be staying in New York?"

"The Plaza."

"Do you know when you will arrive?"

"Not until late Saturday afternoon or early Saturday evening. The studio scheduled a screening Saturday night at eight P.M., so I wouldn't have much time to spare. It would be better if we waited until the publicity mill is rolling and the movie is about to open."

The movies at the junkets in question were big ones, and I didn't know if I should tell the agent any details about them. It was inconsequential to me, but movie companies are very competitive and very secretive. I thought it best to keep my mouth shut.

The agent didn't pursue the issue. She just said, "Miss Zadora was curious." She was very polite about it, and I thanked her, reminding her that I would welcome the chance for an interview when Pia's movie was ready for release.

That Thursday I flew to Los Angeles to interview Ben Kingsley for "Gandhi" for Columbia Pictures, then flew cross-country to New York to interview Jessica Lange in behalf of "Country" for Buena Vista Studio. When I arrived in New York on Friday, I went right to my room, where I was dumbfounded to see an overflowing flower arrangement on the nightstand. The card inside the bouquet said, "To my little Polack. Love, Pia."

My first thought was that my friends at Universal Studios were playing a trick on me, as they were releasing "Lonely Lady." The Universal publicity crew knew me and realized I was pretty square. Paulina, my wife since 1960, was and always would be the only woman for me. An affair was out of the question. I didn't need one to bolster my ego.

I had told my rep, Marianne Mitchell, about Pia Zadora's call, and her only comment was that her company was releasing "Lonely Lady" so she would see to it that I got to interview Pia when the movie was ready for release. I wondered why she knew nothing about the plane-trip offer to go from San Antonio to Houston to Dallas, although it really wasn't unusual for a movie star to have a personal publicist who worked outside the studio. Publicists rarely compared notes. They didn't have time, as studios want them to run at breakneck speed with no outside activities interrupting a pre-release publicity tour. Pia's weekend offer was different, since she was still working on the picture and probably had a day or two off.

I realized all that and still wondered if it was really happening. But I didn't take it seriously enough to consider it one of Hollywood's unsolved mysteries. I was glad to have a chance to talk to Marianne, one of the most thorough publicity reps in the movie business. She's also a good friend, and I knew she wouldn't be upset if I told her about Pia Zadora and the bouquet of flowers.

"No, I didn't plan this thing as a prank," she said, when I asked if she had anything to do with it.

"I haven't even had any meetings with Pia Zadora. Call her hotel and ask her. She'll take the call if you call her husband. He's a Las Vegas promoter and gets calls all the time. She and her husband always stay at the Sherry Netherland, so go ahead and call her."

She gave me his name so I asked for his room and, to my surprise, Pia Zadora herself answered the call. I identified myself and told her I had a bouquet of flowers with a card signed by her.

"Then you got them!" she said with obvious excitement.

"I wanted to greet you in some way, and I still want to meet you. You see, I'm Polish—a Polack like you—and don't tell me you're not a Polack because that will make me very disappointed!"

She was much too friendly for a celebrity, so I wasn't kidding myself about my own importance. All Pia knew about me was my Polish-sounding name, although no one else took my heritage to heart. In fact, most people misspell my name, ending it with an "i" instead of a "y." Even after I spell it out for them.

Pia didn't give me a chance to interrupt her. She talked rapidly, rarely taking time out for a breath. I told her I'm mostly of Polish extraction but have some Russian, Lithuanian, French, and German blood in me. Her only comment: "A perfect blend, but you're still my little Polack and I want to meet you. Are you free this evening?"

"No, I'll be watching a movie in just a few minutes."

"When will you be through?"

"The studio has dinner scheduled at ten-thirty."

"Fine. You can skip the dinner and meet me at my favorite Italian restaurant. My husband will be with me, and you can bring some guests of your own if you want to. You can invite as many as four besides you. We will take you all to dinner."

Wow! Is this woman on the level? That was all I could think about. Trusting she meant what she said, I invited some of my friends, with the warning that it could all be a hoax. But if it was on the level, they would never doubt any of my "personal" stories again. I think all of them hoped it was a hoax so they could hold it over my head.

I invited Roger Downing, my counterpart at the San Antonio Express. He and I got along fine and often compared notes about junkets and personalities. I also asked Lou Gaul, from a Philadelphia paper. We always got together on junkets with his friend, Joyce Persico, from a New Jersey paper, so I called her, too. Then there was Lola Hall from an Oklahoma City TV station. We were good buddies, and she and my wife, Paulina, got along well. All of them readily accepted, and each said he or she would pay for their own dinner if it was a hoax. They were that eager to find out.

We went to the restaurant around 10:20 P.M. It was crowded, but I asked the maitre d' if Pia Zadora had a table, as she had invited us.

"She'll be here, and she always uses the same table. Yes, she called and she said to set the table for five extra guests. She'll be here soon."

Once we sat down we started talking about Pia Zadora and what we should ask her. Her movie work was limited. She got more mileage out of stories about her personal life, as she was married to a man several times her age. Their marriage was exploited in all newspapers and magazines, usually alongside a story about Pia's latest "act." She appeared in Las Vegas shows from time to time.

Bob Polunsky's Flicker Footnotes

We didn't have much time to discuss things in detail. We were interrupted by an older man who walked in from a side door covered with a curtain. He parted the curtains and said, "Come in, Pia. Your Polack is here!"

The expression on everyone's face was priceless. I just wish I had had a camera handy when the door opened and the diminutive actress (she is under five feet tall), came out and greeted me with a hug. I wish I could have had a photo of the expression on my face.

"I'm glad you came. I really wasn't sure if you would or not. I certainly didn't mean to make you think it was a joke, so I got here and waited. I don't meet many Polacks in show business. Tell me, do you speak Polish? Do your parents? Who had Russian and who had French and who had German blood?"

The blood count apparently meant something to her so I answered her without making a fuss over it. I wanted her to take a breath so I could ask her a question or two. The questions wouldn't be very substantial, as I knew nothing about "Lonely Lady." But Pia didn't seem the type to want serious-minded questions anyway. She appeared too bubbly for interviews, but I tried the serious approach to questioning her anyway.

"How important is this movie, 'Lonely Lady'? I know you haven't made any big-budget movies up to now. What led to this one, and does it have a big budget?"

"Yes, I was told it does but I never remember figures. I got this movie by auditioning for it. I'm between commitments in Vegas, so I read for the part and got it. Have you read the book?"

I had, but only because the studio sent me a copy when they announced it as one of the "big ones" of the year. They also said someone else had been signed. Her name was Susan something. I didn't remember. All I could think about was that she couldn't possibly be as sexy as Pia Zadora. Maybe that's why the studio switched to Pia.

"This is supposed to be one of the sexiest movies of the year," she said, and her husband nodded his head in agreement.

"The studio dropped the ball on 'Butterfly," and that was going to be the most erotic movie ever made. It had all the right people in it," he said.

"Besides, it was based on a James M. Cain novel to give it some class with such actors as Orson Welles and Stacy Keach and Stuart Whitman and Ed MacMahon. Pia stole the show as a sexy woman who tries to seduce her own father. But the script and the director dropped the ball. It bombed."

Pia interrupted her husband. She didn't want any post-mortems on the film.

"'Lonely Lady' came along just in time," she said.

"I couldn't resist testing for it. It's going to prove that I have sex appeal. Just wait til you see it. We can discuss it then because I know you wanted to talk about 'Lonely Lady' closer to its release date. I don't mind that. Really. That would make this a business meeting, and it's not at all. It's purely social.

I wanted to meet you and see if we could speak Polish together, but I won't hold it against you if you can't. Introduce me to your friends."

Her wish was very much at my command, and my friends were delighted to meet her. She showered them with trinkets from her films—key rings, matchbooks, ballpoint pens, that sort of thing. Each of us got a sackful before we sat down for a big, delicious Italian meal. Pia ordered for each of us.

"I was on Broadway in some small roles," Pia said. "Did you see 'Applause?' I was in the scene with the waitresses and waiters dancing in a café. It was a group dancing thing that gave me a chance to show off my dancing abilities."

I admitted that I had. Twice in fact. Once on Broadway and once in San Antonio, when the touring company performed at the Lila Cockrell Theater on the Hemisfair grounds.

"You did? Then you saw me twice. I was in that tour, too. See, Miklis," she said, turning to her husband. "If I had met Bob first he might have been my Polish husband!"

She gushed a lot and made more out of my Polish heritage than necessary. There was no question that this dinner was a publicity meeting, but there was no point in embarrassing Pia by saying so.

As far as my friends were concerned, they watched her every move and didn't ask many questions. They spent more time talking to her husband than listening to Pia. Every now and then Miklis turned to me and repeated one of the questions asked him.

"Why did she want to make a movie from a Harold Robbins novel?" I asked. Miklis paused a minute, then laughed rather heartily.

"Because Robbins has the ability and opportunity to write some of the most erotic novels ever published. His books sell in the millions, and every one of them has eroticism written all over it. This could be the most erotic movie ever made. If so, it will be a testament to Pia's sex appeal. She took this part because I wanted her to."

"Besides all that, I have to take a break from performing in Vegas," Pia said, breaking into her husband's conversation without warning.

"You see, I'm pregnant. I'm going to have a baby when this movie wraps up. I don't think I could last in a daily workout in a Las Vegas show at this stage of the game, and I want to make a movie that makes moviegoers ask for more. By the time the film is released and making lots of money, I'll be ready for another one."

In retrospect, I think someone misrepresented the movie to Pia Zadora. She had so much enthusiasm about it, reciting a few words of her screen dialogue here and there and praising costars Lloyd Bochner, Bibi Besch, and Joseph Cali as if they were all top names. Actually, Pia Zadora was the biggest name in the cast even though she had very few film credentials. Her name was known because of her personality, not her acting ability.

The cast also included a small part of an up-and-coming young actor I would interview in about ten years. Ray Liotta played a young thug, and this was one of the rungs of the ladder he was climbing in his show business career.

Pia's comments covered the many foreign-born stars she either knew or knew something about. She talked about Sophia Loren and her much-older husband, Carlo Ponti. "He's much older than Sophia, and I'll bet you thought I was the only actress in Hollywood who prefers older men," Pia said, and I didn't have a comment to make about it.

She also talked at length about her movie, "Santa Claus Conquers the Martians," the 1964 film about Santa and two ordinary mortals taken captive by Martians who hoped they could help them solve domestic problems on Mars. Pia's role was a standout to her (she played one of the Martians). She said the movie was supposed to be a big-ticket item but the studio slashed the budget before it was finished.

All of us talked over food and liquor until midnight. When we got up to leave, Pia stopped us and said we could use her private limousine to get back to our hotel. (Boy! Where was my camera when I really needed it!) She kissed me on the cheek and promised to stay in touch so she could tell me whether she gave birth to a boy or a girl.

The next day the junketeers I knew best were all taking about what became a famous dinner date (in my circles anyway) with Pia Zadora. Several reporters out of the loop asked "who the hell is Pia Zadora?" Others approached me with some textbook questions like, "What does she expect her career to do for her?" "Why doesn't she do more theater work, since she's appeared on Broadway?" "Does marriage to a much older man handicap an up-and-coming star?" "Does she plan to keep the same job schedule after motherhood?"

Each question had an answer that could be picked out of Pia Zadora's comments, or so I proudly told my fellow reporters. Actually, it wasn't a good interview because of all those "fluff" comments about inconsequential things. Since it was a social occasion and Pia and her husband were buying dinner, none of my cohorts asked any serious questions about Pia nor her career. Neither did I. We were mesmerized by the situation, and that's probably what Pia intended. We asked those "fluff" questions to help publicize her career as the leading lady of "Lonely Lady," and that's what this session was all about.

Some of the questions were asked again when I got home. Some of my fellow reporters doubted that it had happened, but I had proof. I carefully kept the bouquet of flowers together with her card. When I took it with me to the TV station and newspaper office, there were more questions. Most of them were fluff questions, just like my actual interview with Pia She didn't take things seriously unless it was a frivolous item of information. I had to admit to my cohorts in San Antonio that—in spite of the opportunity—I never got the chance to ask Pia an important question that would really tell us what she thought of her show business image. It would also have put our celebrity-staged interview in perspective.

"And what question was that?" a newspaper reporter asked.

"I never asked her what her favorite color was."

8.
GEORGE BURNS, A LEGEND IN HIS OWN TIME

SOMETIMES HOLLYWOOD GOES OVERBOARD AND DEFINES "A LEGEND" AS any star who passes away while he or she is still active. They probably said it about Douglas Fairbanks Sr. but let things slide as long as Douglas Fairbanks Jr. was around.

They called Oscar winner Mary Astor a legend, but not until she started doing supporting roles to keep from being forgotten. The point is, it's difficult to find a real "legend" among movie stars because each star is so different from another. I'd call anyone a legend who lasted onscreen more than one generation. And there are few of them around.

George Burns is one of the exceptions. His initial movie career lasted from 1932's "The Big Broadcast" until 1939's "Honolulu." Then he called it quits and did radio and TV sitcoms with his wife, Gracie Allen.

In 1975 his best friend, Jack Benny, was scheduled to costar with Walter Matthau in "The Sunshine Boys" but died before production started. George Burns was contracted to replace him, and it was his first movie since 1939. He had been off the big screen for almost a half-century before he made "Sunshine Boys," and won a Best Supporting Actor Oscar for it. He also became a legend and held the title of Hollywood Movie Legend from 1976 to 1983, when Don Ameche won the title. Like Burns, Ameche made a long-overdue comeback with "Cocoon" in 1983 and, also like Burns, won a Best Supporting Oscar for it.

George Burns made a series of comedies after "Sunshine Boys" and each capitalized on a different facet of his personality. "Oh, God" and its two sequels made the most of his longevity. Who else but the oldest man in show business should play God on-camera? "Sergeant Pepper's Lonely Hearts Club Band," "Just You and Me, Kid," and "18 Again" exploited his close relationship with youth. Young people loved him because he understood their obvious impatience with senior citizens. Although he rarely showed it, Burns himself was irritated and impatient with old-timers. He often joked about it, and young people seemed to follow him everywhere because they were comfortable with him.

The fact of the matter is that George Burns was not necessarily a good interview for those young people. He rambled on and on without waiting for questions, and his style overpowered his talk. He was funny, and he knew it. Arrogance...even innocent arrogance...was part of his style, and that, too, was his undoing. He needed to make more movies that called attention to his longevity in order to grab back the audience that held him in esteem for making "Sunshine Boys."

Burns found such a movie. It was "Going in Style" (1980), a story about three oldtimers (Burns, Art Carney, Lee Strasberg) who didn't like the prospect of getting older. To take the edge off their frustration, they decided to become crooks. Small-time crooks, to be sure, but it put George Burns on the same level as mischievous teenagers as well as envious senior citizens.

"Going in Style" would never have worked without George Burns and his endearing personality. By the same token, George Burns probably wouldn't have been in demand without "Going in Style."

The movie started with three retirees in Queens, where they are completely bored by life. Each anticipated death at any time, so they collectively decided to "go out in style" by robbing a bank. It's something young rebellious people might do, so why not?

The cast was picture-perfect. All three got along quite well, but Burns was still the leader both in the storyline and off-screen. He was the only "legendary performer" in the group and the only cast member asked to go on a midweek junket in Los Angeles to meet the press. The press would be there one night only, and George Burns was the only interviewee. Nobody turned down the studio's request. Not even for just one night in Tinsel Town. My fellow press members and I were going to see and talk to a legend!

The film was screened at the Samuel Goldwyn Theater, where Oscar-nominated films are shown to the voters. It's a large theater decorated with posters of Oscar-winning films. The posters covered all Oscar winners to the present day, meaning there were original posters of "Wings" (1927 and made in San Antonio) to 1982's "Gandhi." As more winners were named, their posters were added to the main floor or the second floor of the theater.

The screen was big enough to be seen comfortably from any seat in the house. For that reason it was often used by the studios to screen their pictures for press junkets. I saw "Star Wars," "Close Encounters of the Third Kind," and the first "Lord of the Rings" at the Samuel Goldwyn Theater. But those were minor spectacles compared to meeting George Burns in person.

As was their custom, the studio screened the film the evening before the interview. The next morning we would meet George Burns at the Century Plaza Hotel, where the TV cameras would roll as each of the invited press members did a six-minute interview with "the legend."

When I was on deck I noticed how energetically George Burns came into the room. He reflected much more energy than I did, but I didn't want to admit it. I blamed the two-hour time difference between California and Texas for making my energy level low. George's energy level was high. It showed in his clothes—a flashy-looking sportscoat, a navy shirt with an open collar, and dark trousers. He also wore sneakers and sported his famous cigar.

"You have the world in the palm of your hand, George," I said in his introduction, and he upstaged me with his line: "That's just because I've been around so long." Then he waved his unlit cigar in my face. "First there was me," he said, "then came Moses. Did you know that I'll celebrate my eighty-fourth birthday this year with this film? I have sixteen years to go. I have some contracts to do a show on my hundredth birthday."

I tried to soft-soap him by saying he looked older in the movie than he does in real life.

"Yeah. They tried to make me look different by thinning out my hairpiece. It looks like you're going to need a little help with hair, too," he said, noting my receding hairline. He also offered me a hairpiece if I needed one ("I've got a whole trunkful!" he said).

"Do you ever wish you could be—say—eighty-two again?"

"Naw. I'm glad I am where I am. In the movie I said that I wish I was forty again, but that was the character talking, not me. It's something I have to get used to because I'm classified as an actor since I won that Oscar for 'Sunshine Boys.' It marked the first time I played a character other than myself in a movie. It was also the first movie I made in over thirty-five years, and it was for the same studio. They must have liked my work or they wouldn't have invited me back." He puffed on his unlit cigar as if to emphasize his comments.

"Your cigar isn't lit, George. Why are you bothering with it? I noticed you didn't smoke in the movie," I told him.

"I haven't smoked a cigar in any of my movies."

He took another imaginary puff on his unlit cigar. "Can you imagine a man my age smoking?" he asked in an incredulous tone. "It would have been unthinkable in any of my movies including 'Going in Style,' and I play a nice old guy who doesn't do anything associated with vice. Not until I decide to rob a bank. I also decide to take the loot to Las Vegas to see how far it will go."

There is more to the movie than that, but the script is pretty shallow compared to the personalities. Burns, Carney, and Strasberg know how to milk a gag until it gets a satisfying laugh from the audience.

George got top billing. He said it was because of his relatively new-found legendary status and nobody—least of all Art Carney and Lee Strasberg—challenged him on it.

"Strasberg was hell to work with," George said matter-of-factly. "I shouldn't say 'hell,' I know. I should just say he is a perfectionist. A drama teacher, you know, and he'd rap me on the knuckles if he didn't think I was doing a scene right. Carney would just belch. I guess both of them were fun, now that I think about it."

Talking about the film gave George an excuse to reminisce about other things in his career. He didn't wait for a direct question to talk about his vaudeville days and tell me a few old-time vaudeville-type jokes. I laughed politely, but I think he knew I didn't consider any of his jokes very funny. But George himself is funny because of his expert sense of timing. He knows when and whether or not he needs to pause and for how long before giving the punchline. He's had plenty of practice over the years, but so have other comedians and I don't know anyone with the sense of timing George Burns has. He knows it, too.

"I started smoking cigars when I was fourteen years old," he said in a slow drawl. "I was in an elevator so often looking for jobs that one guy asked me, 'Do you play anything but this elevator?' It was such a frustrating comment that I took up cigar smoking in earnest just to be able to blow smoke in the faces of guys like that."

George paused and looked at me intensely before adding his next line.

"Can you imagine anyone making a comment like that to a man my age? When I was fourteen, it was okay. But would you believe anybody would say that to me now? [Pause] Well, they look like they might when I get in elevators more than once in the same day.

"I had a crying scene in 'Going in Style,' but you probably noticed," he continued.

"It was easy to cry. I just thought about Jack Benny, a man I dearly loved. He would work so hard trying to make me laugh and get completely and utterly frustrated. On the other hand, I could make him laugh at the drop of a hat. I remember running into him at Chasen's once. He came over to my table and invited me to his. But I insisted he stay at mine. I said, 'Come on over, Jack. Pull up a chair and help yourself to the salt.' It was a dumb comment but it cracked Jack up.

"I was in a doctor's office one day, and a stranger saw me and said, 'It's exciting to sit in an office with a celebrity.' I said, 'It sure is. Who are you anyway?' I got a laugh out of that one.

"I remember the one time somebody saw me and thought I was Jack Benny. He said he was glad to see me and asked how Mary was. I said, 'Fine. I left her in bed this morning.' Then, when he realized I wasn't Jack Benny, he was horrified by my comment.

"'What were you doing in bed with Mary Benny?' he asked with an incredulous tone in his voice.

"I never said I was in bed with her, you did."

George's jokes and comments came in rapid-fire succession, but I really didn't have time to steer away from talk about the movie. As much as I wanted to listen to George Burns reminisce, I politely interrupted him at the first opportunity. But it wasn't easy to interrupt him, because he stayed in gear and went on joke-telling. The fact of the matter was that he couldn't reach a stopping point. That's what made the interview watchable, but I didn't realize it then.

George Burns was really a terrific interview because of his chatter. He would bring up subjects I wanted to bring up, and I realized any more questions from me about the topic at hand would be redundant. George Burns—the legend—was a one-man show, and I was better off if I let him do most of the talking.

I broke the pattern when I changed the topic. It always led to another jokefest with the Legend. Especially when he could reminisce with ease. Like his bogus reputation as a country-western singer.

"I love country music now, but I never used to like it," he said. "The lyrics tell a story just like the ballads used to do in my younger days."

"I'm surprised you didn't sing a country song in 'Going in Style,' George. Surely there would have been a way to lead into one. Don't you see the daily rushes so you can make recommendations to the director?"

"Naw. I never look at rushes because I couldn't change them even if I wanted to. If there was an opportunity to change it, we'd all have to go on overtime."

"Does today's liberal language bother you?"

"As far as I'm concerned, language today is the same as it was yesterday. It's English."

George was hedging. He used some four-letter words in "Going in Style," causing the movie to be rated R. But the producers toned it down because of George's image. They wanted a PG but kept a few minor expletives in the film.

"I worry more about my appearance than my language," he said.

"I can do most of my scenes sitting down these days, but that's a godsend. In fact, they had me sitting down so much I had to go to the men's room to stand up."

Apparently he couldn't resist opening for another one-liner, but my time was running out. I needed to get back on track again.

"Which of your movies do you think Gracie [Allen] would have liked best?" I asked.

"She would have liked all of them. She was in love with me."

A good answer, but I wanted an argument.

"Even the movies that have a downbeat ending, like 'Going in Style'?"

"Sure. Life itself is a downer at times, and 'Going in Style' is a realistic movie."

He had a point there. "Going in Style" was probably the most realistic film in George's current career. It even had a death scene and quite a bit of crying. I let his answer resolve my question without going any further. There was no need to do otherwise.

"Now that you're in your third career—and I mean your current movie career after your radio and TV career—can you say you've done everything there is to do in show business?"

He paused briefly, then came back with a clever quip.

"No. I haven't done toe dancing so I haven't done everything." But he saw a new opportunity to expand his own comments.

"I have danced in movies, though," he said, putting his cigar back in his mouth to signal a pause. He wanted me to ask when.

"I used to teach Polish people to dance, but they wouldn't dance with anyone but me. It wore me out going to all those Polish weddings."

"How do you think movie making has changed over the years, or has it?"

"Well, people look more natural today. In the old days everyone was made up to look like Dolores Del Rio. As far as the art of comedy is concerned, it hasn't changed. But people have. I try to think young. I try to make my jokes sound young even when I talk about the old days. Gracie taught me to do that. She really wasn't a comedienne. She was an actress. A great actress playing a role, and she left the entrances and exits to me. She just filled in with the patter and gave our routines the color they needed."

"Do you spend most of your time working or do you nap a lot?"

"I don't get paid for sleeping. I get paid for staying awake and talking."

"Is your social life active?"

"Of course. I'm not dead yet."

"I remember hearing Walter Matthau rib you about your age during the press conference for 'Sunshine Boys.' Do you mind joking about your age?"

"Why should I? I can still talk about age if I'm young in the eyes of the audience."

I remembered the comment Matthau made to George at that press conference after the press preview of "Sunshine Boys." It proved the wit and "youth" of George Burns. Matthau asked him, "At what age does sex stop?" Without batting an eye, George answered: "It stopped earlier this morning."

Bob, Rodney Dangerfield, Bill Murray, Chevy Chase and Ted Knight at Rodney Dangerfield's New York Night Club.

Ann Jillian planted a kiss on Bob's cheek after her interview.

Robin Williams in a rare serious mood when talking about "Good Morning, Vietnam!"

Jane Withers and Bob Easton were surprise Hollywood guests at Bob's 50th high school reunion.

Dolly Parton sat on Bob's lap for her interview.

Steven Spielberg with Bob and Paulina at a Hollywood Christmas party.

Harrison Ford was always a "Straight Shooter."

Bob got in trouble for putting Meryl Streep's interview in both print and TV.

Paulina and Bob co-hosted a movie cruise with Gloria and Bruce McGill.

Sean Connery talks about James Bond's future.

9.
ROBERT DUVALL, AN ACTOR'S ACTOR

TALK ABOUT ACTORS TO SOMEONE IN THE MOVIE BUSINESS, AND THEY BOW their heads when some names are mentioned. Those names designate "actor's actors," or, actors even the pros respect. They usually do colorful supporting roles and occasionally, a leading role in a low-budget picture. Sometimes they could play a lead in a "Class A" production, but those instances are rare.

Some of the more famous "actor's actors" are Spencer Tracy, Edward G. Robinson, Humphrey Bogart, Tommy Lee Jones, and Robert Duvall. Duvall is a fairly recent addition, and he was about to have his first leading role in a Class A production, "The Great Santini."

"The Great Santini" was based on a Pat Conroy novel of the same name. The title fit the storyline, but no one would know that till they read the book. That's a dangerous thing to do for a movie because the title is the core of all advertising and publicity. Even though the movie would have a multimillion-dollar budget, that title would eventually drag it down.

The studio toyed with such titles as "The Ace" to get a crowd, but nothing worked. Not until a critic saw it at a small art house in New York and praised it to the heavens. He also said it was based on Conroy's book, "The Great Santini." The studio took the hint and rereleased "The Ace" as "The Great Santini" all over the country. This time it clicked and so did Bob Duvall. As the title character, he mesmerized his audience and would never again play a supporting role unless he really wanted to.

I got to meet him before all the flack about "The Ace" or "The Great Santini" took place. It was at a junket to be held on location on Fripp Island, South Carolina, where the film was shot. Fripp Island is a tiny strip of land with a military base. Families of the military lived in tall, clean-looking, white condominiums that were virtually back to back on the island. There were no hotels or motels, so the inhabitants of those condos graciously turned them over to the movie studio for the press people to use.

Most of us were paired up because there were more reporters than condos. Even so, we had some privacy. Every single member of the press had his or her own bedroom. Another bedroom in the condo was for a roommate. My roommate was John Bustin from the Austin Statesman.

He and I weren't strangers. We had known each other for a long time. In fact, John reviewed local stage productions, including those at the University of Texas. It was in the 1950s when my wife-to-be, Paulina Norman, appeared in "The Man Who Came to Dinner" at the university auditorium and got a rave review from John Bustin. In later years Paulina and I would travel with the Bustins on movie trips. But this time John and I were on our own.

We had some testy times because of the equipment. The alarm clock in our condo wasn't working so we were both late for our first interviews. The food supply for the press people was routine fare. We had cold cuts instead of steak, and we had been spoiled by previous junkets when steak was the main bill of fare. But we made the best of it, and—when all was said and done—we realized the interviews were well worth the inconvenience. Especially the interview with Robert Duvall. I had both a print interview and a TV interview with Duvall, and he was completely at ease for both. Fortunately for the interview, his easy manner was contagious.

Bob Duvall is not an imposing man. He could easily blend with the woodwork when he's out of character. But he comes alive when talking about his movie characters, and at this point in time, he was upset because his role as a gung-ho commander in "Apocalypse Now" had been drastically cut. Duvall spoke to me about that film before we got around to "The Great Santini."

"My role in 'Apocalypse Now' was cut and cut badly," he said in a calm but angry-sounding voice. "If it hadn't been cut, I would have been very proud of my characterization."

"Are you blaming [director] Francis Ford Coppola?"

"Who else?"

"Then you wouldn't want to work for Coppola again?"

"Well, I didn't say that." His anger was subsiding and he spoke a bit shyly about his career now. "Francis is a good director so yes, I would want to work with him again."

Actually, Robert Duvall's characterization in "Apocalypse Now" was highly praised in spite of the way it was cut. Coppola himself said Duvall was one of the top three character actors currently working in Hollywood. He was even nominated for an Oscar as well as the British equivalent of Oscar for his role.

That was in 1979. No one then knew that almost a quarter of a century later Francis Ford Coppola would reinstate all the deleted scenes of "Apocalypse Now" and rerelease it as "Apocalypse Now Redux." When the restored version was shown to the press, everyone praised Bob Duvall more than any other performer in it.

But now it was 1983, and I had a different set of questions to ask Bob Duvall. I wanted to find out—among other things—how and why he picked "The Great Santini" for a project. Was it his agent's doing?

"No, I no longer have a Hollywood agent," he said. "I've cut myself off from the movie colony because I want to be very selective. I really prefer stage to screen anyway, but I'll take any role that I feel is worth my while."

"Then you must identify strongly with your character, or was it a chance to be different?"

"Both. The movie is based on Pat Conroy's autobiographical novel, and the character is a tough Marine pilot who prides himself on his aerial acrobatics. That why he's called 'The Great Santini.' It's a play on circus nicknames.

"But he's different in ways you may not suspect. He's tough on his family, forcing them to live by Marine rules with a strictness that makes him a stranger to his family. His son [played by Michael O'Keefe] is too sensitive to cope with his father's strictness. Their confrontation scene is a pivotal point for the movie, and the movie itself is like an accident waiting to happen. There are racial problems, because it takes place in the Deep South when racism ran rampant."

I asked him if he based his characterization on anyone he knew in real life, and he just laughed.

"Not completely, of course, but I have vivid memories of colorful characters and applied them to this character to make him more colorful. All actors do that."

He then told me some things about his own background so I could see his character in the movie the way he saw him.

"I was a Navy brat. My father was a rear admiral who wanted me to go to Annapolis, but I rebelled. Being a career Navy man was not in my plan for myself, so we often quarreled about it. I'm a man of compromise, though, so I asked my father if he would be happy if I studied government in college, and he said he would. I studied government for as long as I could. Before graduation, I switched to Drama and graduated a dramatics major.

"Sandy Meisner was my first director. I attended the Neighborhood Playhouse in New York and acted in plays by Tennessee Williams. Sandy directed all of them, and encouraged me with every play. That's what gave me the confidence to audition for the movie version of 'To Kill a Mockingbird.' I got that role but I couldn't wait to return to the stage to learn more about my craft."

He counts the original Broadway version of "Wait Until Dark" as one of his favorite stage vehicles. He also liked working in "American Buffalo." But I was more concerned with his movie credits.

"Isn't movie-making easier on you?" I asked. "You don't have to repeat the same character and same action night after night like you do on stage."

"True. You just have to repeat the role often enough to suit the director, and sometimes that's pretty strenuous. Acting itself is strenuous, but I like it. I work out in a gym, to keep myself limber so the exhaustion of acting a role doesn't get to me. I also like tennis and canoeing. They are strenuous, too, but they have a way of relaxing you when you're finished."

"Why do you like to take on different roles every time? Is it because of the challenge of doing them or are you testing yourself?"

"Both. I want to see if I can handle a variety of roles, and I've been very much aware of the differences in characterizations that I have to deliver. I've also made some mistakes. There are some movies I'd like to forget."

"Such as?"

"Well, 'The Betsy' was one I would like to forget. It was a trashy movie based on a trashy book, but it gave me the chance to work with Laurence Olivier. The money I received for that movie was good, too."

Duvall played a man who was bitter after he learned his father had committed suicide. He took out his bitterness on everyone around him. The movie's main plot was about an automotive tycoon. The title referred to his dream model of a car. The cast included Lesley-Anne Down, Katherine Ross, and Edward Hermann.

Duvall didn't want to talk about movies he called "losers." He would rather talk about the good ones, like "The Godfather" and "The Godfather, Part Two," in which he played the "Godfather's lawyer" and was the only non-Italian in the "Godfather's family."

Other movies among his favorites include "True Grit" (as one of the meaner cowboys); "To Kill a Mockingbird" (as the character who scared little kids when they went to the 'haunted house'); "The Seven Per Cent Solution" (as Dr. Watson to Nicol Williamson's Sherlock Homes) and "Network" (as William Holden's boss and antagonist).

Three years after making "The Great Santini" Duvall won a Best Actor's Oscar for "Tender Mercies." It was only the second leading-man role he had had, because of his selection process ("It has to be something different"), and he's played mostly colorful supporting roles ever since.

Chief among them are roles in "Days of Thunder" (as Tom Cruise's right-hand man); "Newsies" (as Joseph Pulitzer, newspaper publisher, journalist, and philanthropist); "Geronimo, An American Legend" (as an Indian scout); "Wrestling Ernest Hemingway" (as a retired Cuban banker), and "John Q." (as a detective trying to coax Denzel Washington into releasing his hostages in a hospital Emergency Room).

True to his comments, each and every one was entirely different, and all were portrayed by Robert Duvall, the best example of an Actor's Actor working in today's Hollywood.

10.
HELLO, DOLLY

DOLLY PARTON ONCE TOLD ME THAT "I MIGHT LOOK FALSE ON THE OUTSIDE but everything on the inside is real!"

She knew the impression she made and she knew what image she wanted to project. What's more, she always did a good job of it. That's the main reason why she was a terrific interview. She's my very favorite interview because she sat on my lap for a gabfest. It was when we met to publicize her movie, "9 to 5," and she was dressed to the teeth! I mean she left nothing whatever to a man's imagination, and she knew it.

When she walked into the hotel room, she stopped and looked around, then stopped and smiled when she saw me.

"I think you're just about the sexiest-lookin' man I ever saw!" she said. "Do you mind if I sit on your lap for our interview?"

I assured her she could, and she let out a low yell that sounded like "whoopee!" with a Southern drawl.

Once perched on my lap, she said the one thing that made me blush all over.

"You're really sexy-lookin' and the next time we meet we're going to do something about it, too!"

I was at her mercy after that. She even asked most of the questions—all designed to hype the movie—and answered them before I could stop blushing.

"This is a woman's movie that men can like because it puts ideas in their heads," she said.

"It's all about three secretaries who are tired of being verbally abused by the brute of a boss who makes them serve him coffee all the time," she added, referring to Texas-born Dabney Coleman in his scene-stealing role of the boss.

"They decide to pay him back by kidnapping him and taking over the office, and they do a bang-up job. Now ain't that a laugh?" She laughed to punctuate her comments, then looked at me wide-eyed as if she wondered if I had a comment or had she covered it all.

"I tell ya, I had a blast working with Jane [Fonda] and Lily [Tomlin]. We got along great, and we're ready to work together again on another movie. Do you have any ideas for a movie for the three of us? It can't be a sequel because we wrapped everything up this time. But it would be fun to get together again. Which one of us did you like best in the movie? If it's not me, don't tell me anything!"

She was as bubbly in person as she is in the film, and she's very bubbly in the film. Using her drawl to advantage, she lets her costars know she's game for anything they might want to do to their boss. They tie him up, belittle him, and send away any and all female help who might want to help him. It's the only way they can run the office in peace.

For his part, the boss tries to escape to find a sympathetic cohort to help him corral and punish his three feminine controllers. He finds a sympathetic ear, but the girls have done such a good job of making him look good (as manager of the office) that he can't punish them. It's the best laugh of the picture.

"Did you ever realize Jane and Lily could let their hair down like they do in our picture?" Dolly continued, but she didn't pause for breath.

"I'm telling you, they loosened up completely our first day on the set and we never had a serious moment between us. They're just like home folks to me!"

All of Dolly's maneuvering wasn't in vain. Her constant patter about her good-natured co-stars set the stage for them. I welcomed each of them with open arms and a comment or two about what Dolly had to say about them. You might say Dolly broke the ice for those of us who had to interview the three stars of the show.

Jane Fonda was the toughest. When she wants to, she can be downright cold. But not at an interview session engineered by Dolly Parton! Dolly even welcomed her to the interview room with a friendly "howdy!" and an even friendlier follow-up comment.

"This here sexy-lookin' man is from San Antonio, Texas, the city you were talkin' about just yesterday. You said you've been there lots of times."

What she didn't say was that Jane Fonda came to San Antonio to talk to the soldiers and airmen about the inequalities of the Vietnam Conflict. She got into quite a bit of trouble over it, but I doubt if she confided in her costars. It was past history, and Jane's career was on the upswing after "9 to 5."

Jane Fonda just smiled and nodded and settled in for our interview. After Dolly Parton left the room, her smile faded. Some of her hostility about the Vietnam Conflict returned, but she didn't remember talking to me about it before and wasn't about to start now. Instead, she answered all questions about "9 to 5" with simple statements.

"Yes, I enjoyed working with Dolly and Lily" and "Yes, I would welcome the chance to work with them again" and "No, I didn't think Dabney Coleman's character is true to Texas. He's a caricature!" and "Yes, I think I will be making more movie comedies now because they are so much fun to do."

I was itching to ask her if she remembered flying to Dallas for interviews for "China Syndrome." She had probably forgotten that I was flying up from San Antonio and my plane was delayed. The studio made her wait for me, and she did a slow burn at the time. I remember her asking me if I was the one from San Antonio when I entered the hotel room for that interview. When I said I was, she said, "I was in jail there once. I hate that town!" It put quite a damper on our interview.

If times were different and if I were bolder I might have reminded her that she went to jail because she and costar Donald Sutherland came to San Antonio under the pretense of promoting their movie, "Steelyard Blues." But they really took advantage of the situation to persuade the servicemen in San Antonio to refuse to go to Vietnam. That's when they were picked up, put in jail overnight, then sent back to Hollywood the next day. The real pity of it is that the San Antonio theaters punished their movie for it. "Steelyard Blues" never played San Antonio.

My previous meeting with Lily Tomlin was only slightly tainted. Nothing like my experience with Jane Fonda, however, so I could bring up some facts about it.

"Do you remembering being in the Broadway audience of "Children of a Lesser God" when a strange man sitting next to you told you he enjoyed watching you on TV?"

Needless to say, she didn't remember, and I should have been glad because the guy was me and I always thought Lily Tomlin got up at intermission and never came back because I struck up a conversation with her. But nothing was further from the truth.

I got up the nerve to tell her about it, and she explained it all.

"I grew up with deaf parents so I'm sensitive to their situation. I didn't think 'Children of a Lesser God' presented deafness as objectively as it should have. I just didn't want to see any more of that play under those conditions. It didn't have anything to do with you, and I hope you'll forgive my bad manners of getting up and never coming back. I appreciate your comment—now tell me how you liked '9 to 5'."

We had a pleasant interview as I recall, but no one matched Dolly Parton for personality or effervescence. The closest was Dabney Coleman, the Austin-born actor who played the nerdy boss.

"I had fun with the part. It takes all the sting out of being a wise guy when you poke fun at his image. I can't imagine really acting that pushy and controlling, and I certainly don't abuse any woman, much less her feelings. Doing it in the guise of a fiction character helped me show what it must look like to others," Coleman said.

He went on to say he had a brother living in San Antonio and would tell him to go to the video store my wife and I owned. We specialized in hard-to-get and classic films and had customers from all over the city. Virtually all were adult viewers who wanted to see classic films that were hard to find elsewhere. Dabney Coleman's brother became a good customer of ours.

When the interviews were over, I went to the hospitality room to find Dolly Parton to tell her how much I enjoyed meeting her, but she had already left the hotel. I didn't see her until several years later when she toured the country to publicize "The Best Little Whorehouse in Texas." She was in Austin when I saw her, and she was friendly. It was presumptuous of me, but I would have loved to see a sign of recognition in her face. But it wasn't there. I was just another shy guy who thought Dolly Parton had picked me out of a crowd, so—once again—I was taking myself too seriously. But the memory of her "little scene" with me was etched on my brain. I was thinking good things every time I thought about Dolly Parton, and that was the point she really wanted to make. I couldn't help but be disappointed when she didn't offer to sit on my lap again.

11.
MACHO CLINT EASTWOOD

SOME STARS RADIATE MACHISMO. BEING MACHO IS AN INDEFINABLE QUALITY that causes instant respect and likeability. Errol Flynn was macho. So was Clark Gable. You can feel the vibes of masculinity that surrounded them because it dominated their film roles.

As far as more recent stars are concerned, I'd put Clint Eastwood at the top of today's macho list, with Russell Crowe, Harrison Ford, and Denzel Washington following closely behind. Of all those I've met—and that includes Eastwood, Crowe, Ford, and Washington—Eastwood is the most macho. He is the oldest and most durable of all. He's also the one who explained what macho meant when I asked him.

It was in 1976. Eastwood had just completed "The Outlaw Josey Wales," filming much of it near Santa Fe, New Mexico. The studio decided to have the press junket in Santa Fe so we could breathe in the "macho" atmosphere. It wasn't really a good choice, especially for those of us doing interviews on TV. The wind made too much noise for the microphones, and cameras were constantly on the verge of toppling over. But it gave movie columnists and TV commentators a rare chance to see Clint Eastwood in his natural setting.

He had made a major impact on movie audiences in his Italian-made westerns. He then went back to Hollywood to make a string of inconsequential films before getting entrenched in westerns again. His aim was to direct as well as star in movie westerns, and he established himself fairly quickly with "High Plains Drifter" in 1973 and "The Outlaw Josey Wales" three years later. In between he made some crime melodramas like "Magnum Force," in 1973, to capitalize on the impact he had made as "Dirty Harry" (1971). He was working hard to find his right screen image, and I really felt he was more at home in westerns.

He was living with Sondra Locke while making most of those westerns so he cast her in them. She was a decorative addition but didn't have the kind of personality to compete with Eastwood for attention. She attended the Santa Fe junket but stayed on the sidelines.

After watching the movie, Eastwood hosted a big barbecue at a Santa Fe ranch. He mingled with the press, asking us if we liked the movie and why. As expected, just about all the comments were favorable.

Eastwood played a devoted husband and father who turned vigilante when the bad guys massacred his family. He had blood in his eyes when he went after them, and it was the same kind of blood that fueled his performance years later in 1990s "Unforgiven," the Oscar winner he starred in and directed.

Eastwood established his personality on screen with care. He was the strong, silent type who didn't have to talk much to get his meaning across. Josey Wales was basically the same kind of character as Dirty Harry, only he was a cowboy instead of a cop. At the time, westerns were on the wane with moviegoers.

"People tell me they want the western to return to the big screen," Eastwood said when he was at my table.

"That's one reason why I made 'The Outlaw Josey Wales,' but I'm depending on you guys to level with me. Does it fit in with today's popular movies or not? I've got to know in order to decide what kind of movie to do next."

He was being kind. He already knew what he was going to do next, and we realized it. We decided to tell him what he wanted to hear—that violent westerns hit the right nerves, and that "The Outlaw Josey Wales" had success written all over it.

He thanked us, then asked what we thought about comedy westerns. The answers ranged from lukewarm to mild reactions about comedies. Diehard western moviegoers rarely take western spoofs or comedies to heart. The western genre is too sacred to them, and I had a hunch Eastwood knew it but was willing to go out on a limb and ask anyway.

It wasn't long after the success of "The Outlaw Josey Wales" that he made comedy westerns that costarred him with a chimpanzee. Both "Every Which Way But Loose" (1978) and "Any Which Way You Can" (1980) were successful but not nearly as successful as "The Outlaw Josey Wales." Strong, violent westerns were what audiences of the 1970s apparently wanted to see, and Eastwood was smart enough to keep up with times and attitudes even when he strayed into other genres from time to time.

He asked us more questions than we asked him because he knew where he wanted the interviews to go, and we didn't. I noticed he was never vague with an answer. True to his image, he was forceful and direct.

"Why is it that we don't have more westerns,' I asked, and he didn't hesitate with an answer.

"We do have westerns. I think we'll always have westerns. We just change the setting with the times. Don't you think sci-fi movies are like westerns with different costumes and settings? That's the way I felt about 'Star Wars' and I think most people feel that way whether they admit it or not.

"The basic appeal of 'Star Wars' was its youthful image. Young people fit the sci-fi format more easily. Westerns deal with hardened old guys like me!"

"Do you feel the same way about crime pictures like 'Dirty Harry'?"

"Sure. When one man has to buck the system to see that justice is done, you have a basic western. I made a movie called 'Coogan's Bluff' (1968) to show how old-time western attitudes apply to new-fangled ideas of crime and punishment. It's still an eye-for-an-eye kind of justice, and 'Coogan's Bluff' proved my point."

He followed "Coogan's Bluff" with war pictures called "Where Eagles Dare" in 1969 and "Kelly's Heroes" in 1970. Then he made the first of his comedy westerns, "Two Mules for Sister Sara" (1970). I asked if he would want to make another comedy like it, and he said he wouldn't.

"When I make another comedy western it will have a different mix of characters. I worked well with Shirley MacLaine, but I think she stole that picture with her comedy portrayal of a bogus nun. No one likes to be upstaged, but I respect her for doing it and doing it well."

"In other words, the male macho image has to stay intact for audiences to identify with him. Is that what you're saying?"

"I'm saying I like being called 'macho.' 'Macho' means being a man, and I'm proud to be one."

12.
BEST OF THE BONDS

THE JAMES BOND MOVIES ARE PERSONALITY PIECES AND TAKE A CERTAIN kind of personality to make the image ring true. Sean Connery had it. Roger Moore had it, too, but only up to a point. George Lazenby showed promise but made only one Bond flick, then lost his job because he argued too much with his boss. Connery returned for one more film in the series ("Diamonds Are Forever," 1971) then broke ranks and remade "Thunderball," the fourth in the original series. His remake was called "Never Say Never Again," words that apparently mirrored his previous sentiments as he had sworn he would never make another James Bond flick. But the Ian Fleming book was obviously available to him and whichever studio he worked for. The original "Thunderball" was made by United Artists. "Never Say Never Again" was done by Warner Brothers.

The United Artists producers—owners of all the other Bond titles—replaced Connery with Roger Moore and tried to refashion him in Connery's image. Moore seemed ill at ease at first but gradually got into the swing of things. Once set as James Bond, he couldn't seem to do anything else.

When Moore called it quits, Timothy Dalton took over for two films in the series. But he was too sinister in a role that demanded self-mocking humor. At least, that was the way Sean Connery and Roger Moore had played the character, and they established an image that would be hard to duplicate, much less change. Pierce Brosnan followed Dalton and developed an instant rapport with the Bond audience because he kept close to the original Sean Connery model.

Connery set the mold with sexy lines that came dangerously close to being censored. But Connery could do anything—and he did. He had a distinctive style that was hard to mimic. It was easy to analyze after I interviewed him and noticed that he looked intensely at me when I asked a question. Then, when I was finished, he would lean back and answer authoritatively without taking his eyes off me. He was in complete charge, and we both knew it. He made a total of seven James Bond films, including "Never Say Never Again." Although he made them over a period of years, he never seemed to age. He started out as James Bond and wound up that chapter of his career as James Bond.

Several years later I went back to London to interview Roger Moore for one of his James Bond roles. The studio "updated" the atmosphere for the interviews to differentiate between the Connery era and the Moore era. Sean Connery's interviews had been held in a sedate hotel suite at the Dorchester. Roger Moore's interviews were held at the Playboy Club. The idea was to make Moore seem a lot younger to appeal to a younger generation of James Bond moviegoers.

Roger Moore also had a different style of answering questions. He tried to establish a self-mocking style by pursing his lips and halfway grinning while talking. But he called attention to himself by looking at the camera instead of the interviewer.

Unlike Sean Connery, Roger Moore couldn't adapt his image to other movie roles. He made other movies, but none of them really clicked. He spent many of his early show business years in television with roles in "The Alaskan" (1959); "Maverick" (1961); "The Saint" (1963-1968), and "The Persuaders" (1973). In between he was in a string of lackluster films (most of them as a supporting player) when he was tapped for his first James Bond movie ("Live and Let Die" 1973).

Like Sean Connery, Roger Moore made a grand total of seven James Bond flicks. Also like Connery, he took time to be in other films between James Bond adventures. His movies were very much like those he had made in his pre-James Bond days, only he played the lead instead of a supporting player. Even so, none of them was exceptionally successful.

The lone exception is the cameo he had in the adventure spoof, "Cannonball Run" (1981) with Burt Reynolds. In it he spoofed his James Bond characterization. It worked because it was released when Moore was at his peak at James Bond. His last Bond venture was "View to a Kill" (1985), and he hasn't done much since.

Pierce Brosnan was more like Sean Connery than Roger Moore. That's probably why he had been in the running. He was considered for the role after Roger Moore's swan song. But the producers of his TV series, "Remington Steele," wouldn't let Brosnan go. He had to forgo the chance to be James Bond at the time (Timothy Dalton was second choice), but—once he got fitted to James Bond's shoes—there was no stopping him. He had the gift of self-mockery that Sean Connery had. He also had enough charm to make his conquests in the script believable. His career was enhanced enough for him to make other movies, and he was hailed in some corners as another Cary Grant.

Brosnan was smart enough to vary his characters in non-Bond pictures to avoid being typecast. He could be a colorful villain as in "The Fourth Protocol." He could also be a romantic in comedies like "Mrs. Doubtfire."

Many of his roles were second leads or supporting players, but he became a "star" with "Golden Eye" (1995), his first James Bond film.

Interviewing the Bonds was always fun because of the subject matter, and I was lucky enough to interview Sean Connery, Roger Moore, and Pierce Brosnan when they were at their peak as James Bond.

James Bond is a likable and incurable romantic, and interviewers tend to identify with likeable interviewees. It was certainly easy to identify with Sean Connery. He was an actor who approached movie-making with a businessman's eye. He made no bones about the fact that he enjoyed his work but was making movies for the money involved. Roger Moore never really seemed to like his work but apparently liked the money involved. Pierce Brosnan was more like Connery. He relished his job and made it obvious. You got the feeling that he just expected the money that went with the job.

Even though Sean Connery is more closely identified with the Bond mystique than the other two, he is the only one who outgrew the character but never outgrew his ability to play him. After his James Bond career ended, he earned an Oscar for playing the colorful detective in "The Untouchables" (1987) and went on to play Indiana Jones's (Harrison Ford's) father in "Indiana Jones and the Last Crusade" (1989). I remember interviewing him for the "Indiana Jones" film and talking about his James Bond career. He remembered much of it with relish but disliked the way the producers handled some of the money matters. He said that was the reason he quit the series, as he didn't want to work for those producers any more.

"What would you say if those same producers asked you to come back?"

"I've learned to say 'Never Say Never'," he said. "I even made a movie by that title. But, for now, I'm sure I'd say 'thanks but no thanks.' Besides, I'm too old now."

"What if they asked you to play James Bond's father?"

He grinned widely and paused for what seemed like a long time. But his answer showed he had apparently thought of the possibility before.

"I would consider taking the job," he said. "But it would cost 'em!"

13.
THE JUNKET FROM HELL

NEWSPAPER PEOPLE LIKE TO TRADE "WAR STORIES" ABOUT THE BEST JUNKETS and the worst. A fly on the wall can pick up some real news about the interviewees and, no doubt, would also notice that no two stories about the same interviewee are alike. At least not usually. Every now and then there will be a junket in which all the interviews are "terrific" to every reporter. Then there are junkets in which the line-up of interviewees is unabashedly bad. There's even one that my cronies and I call "The Junket from Hell."

It was in 1992, and the movie was "Under Siege." Martial arts pro Steven Seagal played the hero, and Tommy Lee Jones and Gary Busey were villains. The setting was a 900-foot battleship carrying nuclear arms. Jones and Busey were the bad guys trying to steal the nuclear stuff, but they were no match for the stone-faced Seagal. Especially when he put on a chef's hat in the course of the movie. He not only got his men but also got some unexpected laughs.

Actually, the movie was a pretty good little action picture. But none of the three male stars was motivated to give an exciting interview. Both Seagal and Jones were known as "yep, nope" guys. Gary Busey was just considered an off-the-wall interview. He rarely stayed on course when answering a question, and we thought it was because he had been in a motorcycle accident without a helmet. He fell and hit his head on the curb. Afterwards he was a big advocate for helmets, but the damage had already been done. His interviews were never coherent after that.

The hellish experience started in the studio's hospitality suite as the three male stars were there along with the reporters. Tommy Lee Jones—who was living with his San Antonio-born wife in San Antonio at the time—came up behind me and poked me in the shoulder. Once I realized who it was, I was tempted to raise my hands above my head.

"You're taking my kid through your TV station when we get back home," he said.

"I'd be glad to," I told him. "If you come along."

He didn't answer me directly but handed me his card with a phone number on it. "Call me!" he demanded, then walked away.

The first interview on my schedule was with Gary Busey, and he didn't give me a chance to get a word in edgewise. All he talked about was his motorcycle accident and that he was "untouched" by the fall. He spoke rapidly and didn't even mention the movie. I finally asked if he, Seagal, and Jones were compatible. He looked surprised and just said, "Oh, uh, yeah."

That was our interview. I was learning why this was going to go down in junketeering history as "The Junket from Hell."

Next was Steven Seagal, and I had a list of ten questions to ask. True to form, he answered either "yep" or "nope" to all of them, and I was finished with my questions in less than the authorized six minutes. So I tried to pick out something he could relate to.

"You usually don't show much emotion, but you looked like you were enjoying your role in 'Under Siege,'" I said to him.

"Yeah, well, it's easy to like."

"What makes you say that?"

"My costars were easy to work with. We got along."

"I've heard you always get along well with your costars."

"No, I don't."

"Would you costar with Tommy and Gary again?"

"Sure."

It was hopeless. The junket from Hell was taking its toll on me, but—to use an old phrase—I hadn't seen nothin' yet!

Tommy Lee Jones came into the interview set, sat down, and just stared at me. I looked around but couldn't find anyone who would give me a cue as to when to start and when to stop. Then someone—I never found out who—said, "Speed!" the cue to start talking.

"You apparently like to play a villain in your movies. Is that why you took this role in 'Under Siege'?"

"It's a good role that gives me a lot to do."

"If you were the hero would you have played the role differently?"

"Differently from what?"

"From Steve Seagal's interpretation."

"The director decides that stuff."

"Did the director tell you how to play your colorful character in 'JFK'?"

"Yeah."

I had hoped he would say more about "JFK," as his character was one of the highlights of that controversial film, and he played him expertly. Of course, I didn't know it at the time, but Tommy Lee would win an Oscar within the next two years for "The Fugitive."

When I spoke to him, he seemed ill at ease but confident about his career. His movies had become increasingly better, and it wouldn't surprise me if he won another Oscar in the future. But he apparently needed a script, because he didn't pick up cues to elaborate on any of his answers. Talking to him was interesting but tedious, but I finally fell in the swing of things. I realized the time was dragging on but hadn't looked at my watch when we started so I didn't know how long we had been on camera. There was no one with a stopwatch to tell me it was time to stop, but I felt the interview had gone on long enough. I just ended it myself with, "Tommy Lee, I'll see you back home in San Antonio." He just nodded without smiling, and the interview as over.

I got up and went into the control room to pick up my tapes.

"Nobody gave me any cues," I said to whoever would listen to me.

"Mr. Jones said not to give you any cues," one of the production assistants said. "He said you were going to take his kid through your TV station so we should give you as much time as you wanted."

The mystery of the missing cue-giver was solved! Now I felt flattered. Although it's work to interview Tommy Lee Jones, not just anyone gets unlimited time on him.

There's an epilogue to the story. When I got home, I called the phone number Tommy Lee Jones gave me and left a message. I asked him to bring whoever he wanted to the TV station the following Thursday at 7:00 A.M. I also asked him to confirm the appointment, and someone from his office (or home, I never knew which) called back to confirm it.

The next step was to publicize the fact that Tommy Lee Jones would be my guest on the Morning Show. I figured the publicity would ensure his appearance. Having him on the morning show with the anchor people would also mean I wouldn't have to do all the talking.

Tommy showed up that Thursday morning at 7:00 A.M. on the dot! He came in a school bus filled with kids, and he brought every one of them into our studio.

Once we gathered in front of the camera, I thanked Tommy for coming and asked him to introduce his class of youngsters. He introduced his own youngster and had him do the honors.

Then I showed a film clip from "Under Siege" and asked Tommy if there was anything he wanted to say about his movie as it was opening in town the very next day.

"Yeah. I'll tell people to go see it."

The anchor people and I tried to pry a few more comments from Tommy Lee Jones without much success. But the main task was accomplished: Tommy Lee Jones was a guest star on our show along with his family and friends.

14.
SHHHHH!
MELANIE HAS A MAN IN HER ROOM!

MELANIE GRIFFITH IS A TYPICAL BEAUTIFUL-BUT-DUMB BLONDE IN HER movie roles. Unlike Jean Harlow or even Marilyn Monroe, she doesn't act dumb. She just plays it straight and lets nature take its course. I always discounted her dumb act as nothing more than just an act. That is, until I talked to her at the junket for "Working Girl" in 1988.

Melanie was the "lure" for the press junket for "Working Girl." When studio publicists invite the working press they usually start by listing the participants. Some studios—in this case, 20th Century Fox—were notorious for "promising" personalities who were never even scheduled to show up. They just use their names as a come-on. Fox is often guilty of playing that game, but in the case of "Working Girl," everyone they promised came through. We were to meet Sigourney Weaver, Harrison Ford, and Melanie Griffith at the Plaza Hotel for what studio reps like to describe as "fun and games."

The fun would be trying to figure out if Melanie Griffith was "real" or not. But before we could find out, we were scheduled to do television interviews with Sigourney Weaver—the villainess of this comedy—and Harrison Ford, the hero.

Sigourney played an executive who stole ideas from her underlings when she thought she could get away with it. Harrison Ford played her boyfriend, and he wasn't always in sync with her business methods.

Harrison was my first one-on-one interview for the junket, and I was glad. He is a straight-shooter who never minces words.

"I was asked to play this role even though Mike (director Mike Nichols) knew I didn't do comedy. I'm not that good at it."

"You had me fooled when I saw 'The Frisco Kid,'" I told him.

"That was different. Gene Wilder was in it, and he's a real comic pro. All I had to do was follow his lead. But this time I'm costarring with two women. It wasn't easy to get a handle on my character, but Mike gave me enough leeway to do what had to be done."

Harrison Ford is one of the nicest guys in Hollywood. But he's not known as a good interview simply because he doesn't make small talk. He's not a "yep, nope" kind of guy either. He just answers what he has to and no more.

"I learned how to do a double-take by watching Sigourney Weaver do it," he said when I asked him about it.

"She's good at everything she does. Too bad she doesn't make more comedies."

"What about Melanie Griffith?"

"What about her?"

"Did you learn anything about comedy from her?"

He laughed. "Have you interviewed her yet?"

"No."

"Well, let's talk after you do that interview."

My next interview was with Sigourney Weaver, not Melanie Griffith. It went well, mainly because Sigourney's year was going well. "Working Girl" was her Christmas release. A few weeks earlier she had starred in the drama "Gorillas in the Mist," and she handled both roles beautifully. That was confirmed when she was nominated for Best Actress for "Gorillas in the Mist" and Best Supporting Actress for "Working Girl." Unfortunately, she didn't win either. Jodie Foster won for "The Accused" and Geena Davis won the Supporting Actress Award for "Accidental Tourist" (which also had Sigourney Weaver in the cast). I always felt that Sigourney was slighted. She deserved an award for versatility if nothing else.

Sigourney often said she got roles that Meryl Streep turned down. Whether that was true or not, I don't know. But I do know that Streep was nominated for "A Cry in the Dark" the same year that Sigourney Weaver was up for "Gorillas in the Mist." Neither won, but both did exceptionally good jobs in their movies. As good as Sigourney was as Dian Fossey, the real-life character she played in "Gorillas in the Mist," she was even better in "Working Girl."

"My only other comedy thus far is 'Ghostbusters'," Sigourney said. "But I'd like to do more comedies. Especially if I can land a leading man like Harrison Ford more often. He's the kind of actor who lets a woman react to him, and all my reactions were positive. I could laugh with him because he's basically a very funny guy, but I don't think he realizes it. He's easy to talk to and act with. I learned about comedy from him and he doesn't even consider himself a comic actor."

When I asked her if Melanie Griffith gave her any pointers about comedy, she laughed out loud.

"Melanie is unique. Things seem to come natural to her so she looks and acts like a natural comedienne. Let's just say she lets it all hang out. No, I didn't get any pointers because I'm not a natural comic. I have to work at it."

It wasn't until I finally got to talk to Melanie Griffith that I understood what Harrison Ford and Sigourney Weaver were really saying about their costar.

My interview with Melanie Griffith was in one of those little cubbyhole rooms at the Plaza Hotel, and she was late. The camera crew thought it would be a good excuse to take a break, so they left me alone to wait for Melanie's entrance. When she came in, she started talking immediately.

"I don't want to say anything about Don Johnson," she said before she sat down.

I assured her I had no intention of mentioning him, but that didn't stop her from continuing to talk about him.

"He's in my room upstairs and I don't want anyone to know it."

"That's okay with me."

"You do know who Don Johnson is, don't you?"

I assured her I did. Don Johnson was her former husband. They'd been divorced for a while and the movie magazines were full of gossip about their new affair. The gist of those articles was that Melanie and Johnson would remarry.

"Well, it wouldn't be right for everyone to know he's staying in my room," she continued. "They're already saying he and I will get remarried, but I'm not sure yet."

"What does Don think of 'Working Girl'?" I asked.

"Shhhhh! I told you I don't want anyone here at the junket or the hotel to know anything about my relationship with Don."

"They won't hear it from me."

"Do you think it's bad luck for a girl to marry the same man twice? It's been twelve years since I divorced him."

"I have no idea. I've never even thought about it."

"Well, he thinks we've both learned a lot about life since then. I liked him better than my other husband [Cuban actor Steven Bauer], and I really do miss him."

"You never told me what Don thinks about 'Working Girl'."

"Oh, he hasn't seen it yet. But he'll like it. He thinks I'm good at comedy."

"I do, too. You do a very good job in 'Working Girl.' I thought you developed the comedy side of your character with a lot of understanding."

"Why, thank you. You must understand a lot about women. Are you married?"

"My wife and I are planning our twenty-ninth anniversary this next year."

"Twenty-nine years! Now, that's a lot. Don and I were only married for one year."

I was beginning to see what Harrison Ford and Sigourney Weaver meant about Melanie Griffith. She is funny, and the best thing about it is that she doesn't even realize it. She just says whatever comes to her mind, like a child.

It's odd that more directors don't cast Melanie Griffith in comedy roles. She was Oscar-nominated for "Working Girl" in 1988 but didn't make another comedy until the remake of "Born Yesterday" five years later.

"Born Yesterday" was a flop, mainly because Melanie Griffith tried to act just like Judy Holliday did in the 1950 version when she won her Oscar. Melanie would have been better had she just acted herself, just as she was doing in our interview.

Her track record in both movies and marriages is not enviable. She remarried Don Johnson not long after "Working Girl" was released, and the marriage lasted longer this time. They were still married when they costarred in the "Born Yesterday" remake in 1993. But they split soon after, and Melanie played the field for awhile. She finally married again, this time to Spanish heartthrob Antonio Banderas. To the best of my knowledge, they are still married, but I haven't seen Melanie Griffith onscreen or off for quite awhile.

Our interview for "Working Girl" is still vivid in my memory. I remember when it was over and we said goodbye. I turned to her and halfway-whispered "Give my regards to Don!" She looked shocked, and then said, "Shhhhh!" very emphatically, adding, "I told you not to mention him. Nobody knows he's in my room and I don't want them to!"

"Don't worry," I told her. "Your secret is safe with me."

15.
RODNEY DANGERFIELD
FINALLY GETS RESPECT!

ONE OF THE COMMON JOKES AMONG MOVIE COLUMNISTS AND REVIEWERS IS Rodney Dangerfield. He has played one serious role, and it was the melodramatic father who made sexual advances to his daughter in 1994's "Natural Born Killers." All his other movie characters are self-deprecating comic caricatures. They are self-conscious comedy characters who act as if they know why he "gets no respect." He makes the most of his tagline by asking for disrespect in his movie characterizations. The sillier the character, the less respect he gets.

There is an exception to that rule, and I witnessed it at the press junket for "Caddyshack" (1981) in which Rodney Dangerfield costarred with Chevy Chase, Bill Murray, and Ted Knight. To make sure he—and his character—got some kind of respect, Dangerfield convinced the studio to hold the press junket at his night club on First Avenue in New York. It would give the press people a chance to see it, since it was closed in the daytime and daytime is when the press people congregated inside for a press conference with the stars.

Reaction to the movie was mixed. It often is when it comes to raunchy comedy even though "Caddyshack" had some moments of high comedy. Still, it was considered "low comedy" by purists.

Critic Judy Stone from San Francisco as much as said so with her first question. She asked the cast members why they saw fit to emphasize "tits and ass" humor.

Chevy Chase was the first to respond. He said, "Do you have something against tits?" and his cohorts chimed in with equally cynical comments.

As the title suggests, "Caddyshack" was an irreverent picture about golfers who take themselves too seriously. They are balanced by golfers who don't take anything seriously. Rodney Dangerfield set the tone with a golf sequence at the beginning that established all the references to be spoofed. Chevy Chase followed as a golfer who takes his game as seriously as he takes himself. Bill Murray played the grounds keeper who had a continuous fight for supremacy with a gopher. The movie was pure corn but had the cast to make it work.

Most of the questions leveled at the cast members were either hooted down or ridiculed. Most of us sat back waiting for it to end so we could look in all the nooks and crannies of Dangerfield's nightclub. Those of us scheduled to do some TV interviews were frantically trying to assemble a few logical questions to ask this manic cast. I never did get a suitable list so I decided to wing it. It seemed the only practical thing to do when interviewing Chevy Chase, Bill Murray, Ted Knight, and Rodney Dangerfield at the same time.

The interviewees sat in chairs arranged in a semicircle around the interviewer. It was a not-too-subtle way of making the interviewer feel as if the comedy group was closing in on him or her. Brian Doyle-Murray (Bill's brother) was also on hand, as he wrote the script and had a small role in the film.

The interviewees pretty much ignored all the questions asked. They talked among themselves, threw barbs at the interviewer, kidded Ted Knight unmercifully, and generally acted silly. It was almost like an extension of their movie characters, and they seemed to have a good time—mostly at the expense of the interviewer if he or she tried to ask a serious question.

I didn't want this to happen to me so I decided to start off with a somewhat silly question to Bill Murray. "Were your comments to the gopher mostly ad libs, Bill? I mean no one would expect your dialogue was actually written out for a movie like this."

"Oh, they wouldn't, would they?" came the response, and it was from scriptwriter Brian Doyle-Murray. He came onto center stage and grabbed me by the collar as he said it. I was shocked, and it showed. It also got a good laugh when I showed it on TV.

Doyle-Murray ended his staged tirade with a few choice remarks at Ted Knight that questioned Knight's masculinity. It was risqué but not risky. The cast members and the press people knew better than to take such ribbing seriously. I still felt a little sorry for Ted Knight. He wasn't fielding things very well.

"Ted?" I asked. "After the way these guys treat you, do you really want to play with—I mean, perform with—these guys?"

Everybody laughed as Ted Knight answered in a loud voice that could be heard over the laughter. "I'd consider it a great honor to both play with and perform with these guys," he said.

The interviews were only about five minutes long, but I got about an hour's worth of replay value out of my segment.

16.
CRUISING DOWN THE CARIBBEAN WITH LENNY

PAUL MARKEY, MY COLLEGE ROOMMATE, CALLED AND ASKED IF I'D BE interested in hosting a Movie Cruise. He wanted to get me together with the cruise line and travel agency planning one.

It sounded good, depending, of course, on what was expected of me. So I met with Paul and the cruise line people to discuss it. They had it all planned out. They wanted me to furnish a Hollywood celebrity, movie trivia questions and prizes for the winners, and some movies—preferably first-run—to show aboard the ship while we were at sea. In return, Paulina and I would have a free cruise to the Caribbean for a week, airfare to the port of departure included.

I had never been on a week-long cruise before, and my wife wanted to go. This was a project that I never dreamed would happen, and that alone made it a challenge to resolve. If I could do what the cruise line people wanted, we would have a vacation unlike any other we'd ever had. So we made a list of what we had to do.

The trivia questions would be easy. I do that all the time anyway. Getting the prizes might not be so easy, so I called the various film companies and asked if it was possible to get any of the T-shirts, caps, key rings, and other items they pass around at press junkets. Each of the eight film reps promised to try, and each came back with the same answer: They could send me the leftovers from the press junkets, and assured me there always were leftovers around. I accepted the plan, gratefully.

Getting a new movie would be harder to come by. Movie studios want a big audience for "sneak previews" as well as premieres. The audience of official moviegoers at a Movie Cruise would probably be around a hundred. At least, that's what the cruise line projected, and that wouldn't be enough to satisfy the film studios. Besides, showing it aboard ship meant it was no longer "first-run product" by the time it got to theaters, and movie houses would use that as a means of taking a discount.

Things would be different if I were a national critic or a well-known Hollywood figure. It would even be different if I had a top-name

Hollywood celebrity to go along. It wouldn't be easy to get a guest celebrity, but I would try.

The first celebrity I asked was John Goodman, and he was interested. But he sent me to his agent, and that was a big stumbling block. No press agent was about to book his or her best client unless some money changed hands. Agents get ten percent, and the cruise line didn't want to pay anything. How do you get "name" people to go without paying them for the use of their name? You can't in this business unless there was an angle of some kind. The only thing I could think of was to invite celebrities I knew from Texas, preferably from San Antonio, and there were plenty of them.

At the time "Twin Peaks" was a popular TV series, and one of its stars was Lenny von Dohlen, an actor from Goliad, Texas, who came to San Antonio often. Lenny wasn't widely known, but his face was familiar because of "Twin Peaks." Besides, I knew him, so I called his family in Goliad and asked how to reach him. They gave me his Hollywood phone number.

I explained to Lenny that the cruise line didn't authorize a talent fee, but the entire cruise would be free for him and whoever he wanted to take along. He would get first-class air transportation to the port of embarkation, and everything else was absolutely free. All he had to do was let me interview him in the ship's theater in front of the passengers, then mingle with those passengers so they could say they met a real-life movie star. He was hesitant at first but agreed with the proviso that he had the option to cancel out if a movie job came along.

"I've been tied up with 'Twin Peaks' and don't anticipate a movie role coming along, though. Frankly, I could use the rest and relaxation.

"Besides, it would be a good chance to spread the word about 'Twin Peaks' and the few movies I have to my credit."

I asked if he would bring along a movie or some episodes of 'Twin Peaks' suitable for a family audience. It would help introduce him to the group but also count as one of the movies I was to furnish.

Lenny agreed, but I still had to get some more movies. I called around, beginning with movies made for TV. HBO was very helpful. So was Turner Classic Movies. Both had some original made-for-TV movies and said they would get me ones that were due to play during the time of the cruise. It would be good advertising. It was also advertising they didn't have to pay for. The cruise was to Puerto Rico, the Virgin Islands, Jamaica, and a privately owned island close to Haiti where the cruise line would have a day-long barbecue. The line-up sounded fine, especially since it would be a first-time Caribbean cruise for Lenny as well as for Paulina and me.

Lenny is a very nice guy, but he's basically shy and doesn't like to be the center of attention. He was a good sport about it, especially when I interviewed him in front of the cruisers. He is one of the most intelligent people I have ever interviewed, and he graciously talked about his various movies and TV ventures with just enough modesty to make his comments charming. He was, to put it mildly, a "hit"!

Paulina and I celebrated the cruise by hosting a cocktail party in our suite. It was strictly on us. The cruise line didn't authorize it and wasn't about to pay for it. But it was something we wanted to do. It was also a way for the cruisers to tell Lenny goodbye. Most of those who lined up to tell him how much they enjoyed cruising with him were young women. They all had their eye on Lenny, and I'm sure they stayed tuned to "Twin Peaks" first-run and/or re-run every time he was on the show.

When the cruise ended, Lenny, Paulina, and I toasted one another by saying, "Wait till next year!" Since the cruise was a success, we were all eager to see where to go and what to do for next year, and the cruise line was willing. They even asked Lenny to sign a paper agreeing to come along under the same conditions. Those conditions still included the provision that he wouldn't go if a job came along, and it did. By the time we planned the next year's cruise Lenny was committed to direct a play in Los Angeles. We all wished him well, but we would miss him.

At the same time, we didn't have much time to think about it. It was back to Square One for the cruise and the planning had to start all over again.

17.
HOLLYWOOD'S PROFESSOR HENRY HIGGINS

WORD ABOUT OUR MOVIE CRUISE SPREAD FAST. NO ONE ELSE IN SAN Antonio was successful in forming one, but we managed to keep ours going. We even got a Hollywood celebrity who once claimed San Antonio as his home town.

His name is Bob Easton, and I knew him in high school when he went by the name of Bob Burke. He was a former Quiz Kid in Chicago when he was a youngster. By the time he moved to San Antonio and went to Jefferson High School, he was considered a mathematical genius.

Bob was taller than any other guy in high school, and he looked as if he were still growing when I saw him again. He had moved to Hollywood and had a recurring role in the "George Burns and Gracie Allen TV Show." He played Ronnie Burns' buddy, and he was a comic delight with his slow Southern drawl—which, incidentally, was completely natural. He just talked that way, and it qualified him for movie roles when a Southerner or a western hillbilly was needed.

He had featured roles in Abbott and Costello's "Comin' 'Round the Mountain" and in Audie Murphy's "The Red Badge of Courage." In time he developed another, more dependable job in the movie business: He would hire himself out as a dialect coach, and he was very good at it. He became known as "The Professor Henry Higgins of Hollywood" and coached virtually every name star who needed help developing his accent. Bob was as good with words, dialects, and enunciation as he was with mathematics.

I hadn't seem him in several years but always told my friends that I went to high school with him when he appeared on the movie screen. When we planned our fortieth high school reunion, I called him in California and invited him to come and he did.

He asked me to get a hotel room for him and his wife, June, and to make sure it had a king-size bed because of his height. It was a problem, because the small residential hotel the Reunion Committee used for out-of-town guests had a limited number of king-size beds and all were in use. I told Bob he could stay with us, and this bothered Paulina because none of our beds were of the king-size variety. As it turned out, the hotel came through at the last minute.

Bob was a hit at the reunion. Everyone in our class remembered him and he seemed to remember everyone there. Even though he was a member of our class, he was like a visiting celebrity. He was just perfect as a guest celebrity for a Movie Cruise to Bermuda. I invited Bob, and he didn't hesitate. He and June were ready to go.

At the time he had finished coaching the stars of "Working Girl" and had a "cameo" in the finished product. It was the rule of the game. If Bob Easton coached the stars in a particular movie, he also acted in it.

In "Working Girl" he played the radio station tycoon who bought the programming idea Melanie Griffith had (and that her boss, as played by Sigourney Weaver, tried to steal). He made a perfect Southern gentleman with his white goatee and snow-white hair. In fact, he stood out over Melanie Griffith, Harrison Ford, and Sigourney Weaver. That's what the Movie Cruisers told him when we went to Bermuda.

Bob was and is a true celebrity and knows how to handle a crowd. Our interview went over well, and everyone involved in the cruise had a chance to shake Bob Easton's hand.

A few years later our class celebrated our fiftieth reunion, so I called Bob again. He was happy to come in, and once again was the hit of the weekend. This time he helped get actress Jane Withers to serve as a guest celebrity for our reunion.

18.
BAGGING BAGGER VANCE WITH BRUCE

ONE OF THE LAST PRESS JUNKETS I WENT ON WAS FOR "LEGEND OF BAGGER Vance." It was important for me to go because my old San Antonio buddy, Bruce McGill, would be there. He played the important real-life golfer Walter Hagen in the movie about fictional Bagger Vance, a one-time promising golfer (played by Matt Damon). He wanted to make a comeback and become the legend of the title. He's goaded into challenging egotistical Walter Hagen as well as the more mild-mannered Bobby Jones in a tournament. It's a leisurely paced movie, but the pace (as directed by Robert Redford) suited the style of the movie.

The press junket was held in New York with Redford, Matt Damon, Will Smith (who played a ghostly "advisor" to the golfers), Charlize Theron (the romantic interest), and Bruce in attendance. We would interview each of them in a round-table discussion with reporters from different cities asking them questions. We had about twenty minutes per celebrity, and Bruce was about the third interview for our group.

When he came in and saw me, he grinned widely and gave me a bear hug that took me off-guard. Bruce is a big guy, and his bear hugs are stronger than friendly embraces.

"Bob's a home town boy," he explained to the other junketeers, then sat down and dutifully answered questions. He was so glib and forthright that I knew he would be a made-to-order cohost for my Movie Cruise. When I asked him about it, he graciously accepted. Once we were on the cruise I asked him to be a witness for a wedding ceremony. Paulina and I were celebrating our thirty-third anniversary on this cruise and the ship's captain was going to give us a reception.

Bruce was a much different cohost from either Lenny von Dohlen or Bob Easton. He took the time to entertain the Movie Cruisers with background stories from his movies and TV shows. He was easily recognizable because he's been in many popular films. His best-known film is "National Lampoon's Animal House" (1978) in which he played D-Day, the mustachioed motorcycle rider who drove his cycle up the stairs of the Tri-Delta

Fraternity House. He also stopped on the stairs and played "The William Tell Overture" by thumping his fingers against his throat. It became a trademark routine to him, and he repeated it for the Movie Cruisers.

He also showed some experimental tapes that he had done and apologized for the language he had to use in it. No one seemed to mind. They enjoyed the tapes, and they enjoyed Bruce.

Bruce McGill is the only cohost who was on deck more than once. He loved going on the cruises and even flew in from a movie location to take part in one cruise midway through. In time he brought his mother as well as his father-in-law on one of the cruises and they were like "home folks" to the rest of the cruisers.

He was also one of the most casual dressers we had on any of our cruises. He wore short pants everywhere except the dining room, and he took part in several of the off-ship excursions with other Movie Cruisers. Like Lenny von Dohlen and Bob Easton, Bruce McGill was a hit. Passengers on the Movie Cruises still get a kick out of spotting all three of our guest cohosts on the screen. There isn't a week that goes by that I don't hear from at least one of the Cruisers about them.

19.
YOU AIN'T SEEN NOTHIN'S YET!

SPECIAL EFFECTS HAVE BEEN A VITAL PART OF MOVIE-MAKING SINCE THE silent days. But no one ever dreamed they would reach the peaks that they did with the giant tidal waves of "The Perfect Storm," the undercurrent of throbbing sounds of "Sensurround" in "Earthquake," and the realistic look of long-extinct dinosaurs in the "Jurassic Park" movies.

These are just some of the examples of special-effects workmanship that slowly and steadily became the main attraction in today's movies. The characters and their relationships have taken a back seat, and that can and does work against the success of a picture. Audiences need to know enough about the characters to identify with their emotions and care about them. It's really the only way to care if a character survives a special effect or not.

But special effects of all kinds were the topics of conversations about movie-making when Sean Connery, Natalie Wood, and Martin Landau filmed "Meteor" in 1979. It wasn't a great movie because the script was slow-moving and dull before and after the special effects. But the actors were good enough to rise above it through sheer personality.

Director Ronald Neame formatted the film to show the likable characters in danger. Then he let a meteor hurtling towards Earth do its damage.

Samuel Arkoff, Chairman of the Board of American International Pictures at the time, was an experienced movie promoter. He had a knack for knowing what audiences liked and knew how to exploit it. About a dozen years after "Meteor," Arkoff wrote his autobiography with the self-explanatory title of "Flying Through Hollywood by the Seat of My Pants."

He made "Meteor" in 1979 and promoted it as a twenty-fifth anniversary picture for American International. He had cofounded the studio with James H. Nicholson and made a fortune with such films as "Attack of the Crab Monsters," "Humanoids of the Deep," and many Technicolor horror films based on Edgar Allan Poe's stories. After making "Piranha" in 1978, he wanted to add some star-studded "class" to his movie-making and settled on "Meteor" with a big-name cast. He also employed every special-effects expert he could find and was successful enough to keep making special-effects films until he sold the studio to Orion Pictures in the 1980s.

Arkoff did something else that was different. He invited members of the press to visit the set of his new movie and watch it being filmed. Most press junkets are held after a movie finishes production. Thanks to producer Samuel Arkoff, we were going to see a special-effects movie in production.

"Creating special effects is expensive and trying," he said during an interview on the set.

"But we had to make them effective so none of the anticipation in the audience would be in vain. It had to be worth the expense and the frustration even though things don't always come off the way we wanted. But we learned to 'make do,' as you'll see when the cameras start to roll. You'll watch the actors talking about the disasters in the movie. The actual disasters will be handled by special-effects teams so you won't see them til the movie comes out. I just hope the actors make you want to anticipate those disasters."

Arkoff spoke with authority. He knew how to charm interviewers as well as audiences. For example, he was the only member of the production staff who wore a business suit on the set. Arkoff's suit made it clear that he was in charge. It added the right emphasis to his comments, and he always spoke in the first person plural. It made us realize he was also part of the production team.

"We use every calamity we could think of to peak audience interest in this movie, and we intend to advertise those calamities well in advance of the movie's release to get word-of-mouth going," he said.

"The meteor hurtling through space causes a major tidal wave as well as an avalanche. We decided to add some disasters of our own making, like a traumatic parting of the Hudson River in which the muddy river bottom seeps into a moving subway train full of passengers. It was one of the most difficult effects so it had to be planned and executed with care.

"Every device known to Hollywood had to be used, but there aren't many experienced special effects men around. We started from scratch and wouldn't let go until we were satisfied with the results."

Arkoff's ideas made the cast work harder to create personalities that could compete with and—with extra effort—dominate the special effects of the film. He was determined to make "Meteor" the "disaster film to end all disaster films" and his hand-picked cast earnestly wanted to live up to that image if it was at all possible.

Sean Connery knew how to cope with special effects. His experience in the James Bond films had made him a bigger-than-life personality, but even Connery had problems with "Meteor."

"My biggest problem was trying to make the mud scene in the subway look realistic," Connery said, mopping his brow. The hot Arizona sun made him sweat. But he dressed as comfortably as he could, wearing Bermuda shorts and a loose-fitting sport shirt. The sweat showed only on his brow. He was neatly covered with a hairpiece to hide his receding hairline.

"I went to the hospital with a bronchial infection after doing that scene," he added. "Now I feel that I've gone through enough disasters. But it stands to reason that there'll be more. The disasters will make the film work so the more the better. I feel the worst is behind me, but we'll see what else Sam [Arkoff] has up his sleeve."

Natalie Wood agreed with Connery. Even though the stars were probably coached, they spoke with enough sincerity to make their comments credible.

"I know Sean is right about the special effects," she said.

"Movies are made to entertain with bigger and better things all the time. The movie audience that buys tickets to see 'Meteor' wants to see things they haven't seen before."

Unlike Connery, Natalie Wood looked as fresh as a daisy. The intense heat didn't seem to bother her at all even though she wore long hair that must have been warm on the back of her neck. She didn't even brush her hair aside, perhaps knowing that her hairstyle let her natural beauty show through. She wore a loose-fitting dress that looked breezy enough to make her look fresh all the time.

"I hope 'Meteor' shows people the latest ways to twist Mother Nature around Hollywood's little finger. But—as an actress and as a woman—I would have liked to see more development of the romantic aspects. It's a little disheartening to realize that people will go to see a disaster quicker than they'll go to see me kiss Sean Connery! But it shows how much moviegoers have changed over the years. Glamour is a by-product of movies and no longer a visual ingredient."

Natalie Wood was the most cheerful interview of the lot. When I asked her to autograph a picture of herself for me, she wrote, "To the other Bob in my life. Natalie Wood." It was a nice gesture that made me like her even more. I even wished her husband, Bob Wagner, had been on the set to see the inscription.

Martin Landau was also on hand and was very businesslike with his interview. Like Sean Connery, he wore Bermuda shorts to keep cool. He also wore a T-shirt instead of a sportshirt.

"The studio wanted to make a picture that would outdo Hollywood's most sensational epics," Landau said. He spoke rapidly so it wasn't easy to get every word. I had to ask him to repeat his comments.

"Our director [Ronald Neame] wanted to outdo himself. He made 'Poseidon Adventure,' you know, and he knew the public expected him to exploit disaster in his movies.

"Some people just go to movies to see disasters these days. At times I do, too. I felt that way about 'Space 1999,' my syndicated TV series. I knew the viewers wanted to be lured to the brink of disaster vicariously. When you identify with the character on the screen you also go through his emotional experiences. When he goes through an avalanche, or when he weathers a storm, or when he has to see the entire world almost come to an end—well, we go through those things with him. That's part of the fun of going to the movies.

"We all know that many movies don't affect people emotionally, and it's a remarkably satisfying emotion to be frightened to death and still walk out safe and sound once it's over."

The "Meteor" press junket was one of those few junkets that allowed time for the press people to be on their own. None of them do so any more as several film companies now "piggy-back" one another so the press sees several movies and attends several interview sessions until it's time to fly home. There's no such thing as "free time" any more. When there was, we often made the most of it. Especially in Flagstaff, Arizona, when we saw "Meteor" being filmed.

Six of us got together and rented a car so we could drive to Sedona to see the famed canyons there. We weren't sure how to get there, but we intended to drive until we saw something that looked like a canyon, relying on some maps that looked weathered and worn. Actually, those maps weren't very helpful, making all of us pretty frustrated. After driving for about an hour after nightfall, we stopped at a gas station to ask for directions to the Sedona Canyon.

"You just drove through it, buddy!" the attendant said.

I had driven a narrow, rocky road all the way to Sedona with bright lights that upset drivers coming toward me. I didn't flinch when they yelled obscenities and turned their bright lights back on me. It was a twisting, turning drive that exhausted all of us. We didn't realize that we were driving through the actual canyon and not alongside of it. We had actually been on the brink of disaster but didn't realize it!

If we hadn't talked to Arkoff, Connery, Natalie Wood, and Landau we wouldn't have realized the drama of our own situation. They told us in graphic terms what we should feel after going through an emotional experience at the movies. We went a step further by driving on the brink of disaster in real life.

20.
CAMEOS—THE WOMEN

I'VE TALKED TO DOZENS—MAYBE HUNDREDS—OF ACTRESSES OVER THE years. I've been at this game since 1953 and still talk to stars on occasion but not nearly as often as I used to. Every time an interview comes up, I think about those very special interviews—those with stars who gave me something to remember them by.

Like meeting Genevieve Bujold at the Los Angeles International Airport. She was ahead of me in line at the ticket counter, and I almost didn't recognize her. She wasn't wearing makeup and wasn't dressed like a movie star. She had baggy pants and an oversized jacket and blouse, and looked like a teenager on Spring break. But there was something about her face. I could not resist asking her if she was Genevieve Bujold, and, sure enough, she was. She was downright friendly, too. I remember her opening words: "Look at me! Don't I look like a mess? Well, I believe in comfort when I travel!"

Sandy Dennis was another star who "believed in comfort," and her definition was very unusual. She came to San Antonio to appear at the Fiesta Dinner Playhouse. I forget which show, but that's not the issue. Stars who toured with dinner theaters were usually on the way up or on the way down. Sandy Dennis—who won an Oscar for Best Supporting Actress in "Who's Afraid of Virginia Woolf?" in the mid-1960s—was on her way down. She hadn't made a major movie in years when she came to the Alamo City.

As was the custom at the time, I was invited to interview the star of the Playhouse productions over lunch, and it was always at a restaurant the star selected. Miss Dennis picked La Louisiane, San Antonio's swankiest restaurant at the time.

I expected her to be dressed to the teeth for the occasion, but she wasn't. When I walked in she was already seated with her agent at the table, and I didn't recognize her. She wore a skirt that resembled a hoop skirt, and had an old-fashioned bonnet on her head. She didn't have any makeup, and her blouse had long sleeves that seemed to engulf her.

She explained her appearance by saying, "Do you like my new outfit?"

I nodded and she said, "I bought it at Goodwill this morning. You'd be amazed at how many clothes at Goodwill have a lot of wear left in them!"

I don't remember anything about our interview. I was too astonished at her get-up and her attitude about it.

Then there was the time Dorothy Lamour and I were guests on the same radio program. She was in San Antonio at the time for a performance at the Fiesta Dinner Playhouse—I believe it was "The Girl Friend." I was the weekly "movie trivia player" on the Mary Denman-Carl Wiglesworth Show on a local radio station. The cohosts usually had me stay past my trivia time to interview their guest celebrity along with them. It worked out fine because I was able to make small talk with the celebrity during commercials.

"I'm going home to New Orleans right after the dinner theater engagement, but I don't want any fuss made about it so don't tell anyone you might know in New Orleans." Dorothy Lamour said.

She apparently thought her information was more important than I did because her "small talk" consisted of long sentences. I assured her that I wouldn't tell a soul because the only person I knew in New Orleans was the movie critic for the daily paper.

"Oh? You know him?"

"Yes."

"Well, don't call him and tell him I'm coming."

I told her I wouldn't.

"People like to gawk at celebrities, and I don't like it," she said, crossing one leg over the other. I noticed she wore a slit skirt that revealed thighs that weren't as slim and shapely as they were during her Hollywood heyday.

"When I go home, I want to relax with close friends. I've spent my life in the limelight. Now I want out of it."

She hadn't made a movie in many years but was prominent in the dinner theater circuit. At one time she traveled all over the country to help promote her musicals as well as the popular "Road" pictures with Bob Hope and Bing Crosby.

"I was disappointed that Bing and Bob didn't want me for the third lead in 'Road to Hong Kong,' the last 'Road' picture. I know I'm older now, but so are they!"

Hope and Crosby cast her in a cameo role under her own name. The actual female lead was Joan Collins. Anyway, the movie didn't fly and most people—including me—think it was because the boys didn't utilize Dorothy Lamour the way they had in previous "Road" pictures.

She also came to San Antonio to introduce a showing of "This Is the Army" at the Majestic Theater in the 1990s. It was a reissue to salute the San Antonio USO and the many military bases we have here. Dorothy Lamour was invited because she reportedly sold more war bonds than any other movie star during World War II.

I met Ginger Rogers twice, and both times were when she was on a public relations tour. The first time she was here representing J.C. Penney, as she was their "fashion consultant." I interviewed her "live" during a TV newscast, and she did a lot of posing. She also pulled her cheetah-skin coat snugly over her shoulders.

At the time we were taking "live" phone calls to the visiting celebrity, and a woman called and asked Miss Rogers if she wasn't ashamed to wear a coat made with the skin of an endangered species!

The second time was when Miss Rogers was a special guest of our friends, Bobby and Maggie Sheerin. They hosted a dinner for her at the Menger Hotel, and Paulina and I were among the guests.

Paulina took along the book "The Films of Ginger Rogers" and asked her to autograph it.

"I should say not!" was Miss Rogers's answer. "I didn't make any money off that book. The author didn't even thank me with a check!" she said.

I also interviewed Margot Kidder live and asked for questions for the listening audience. A woman called and asked, "Miss Kidder, are you married?"

"No," she answered very smugly. "But I am knocked up. I have a live-in boy friend."

The switchboard lit up like a Christmas tree.

Tina Turner is an explosive personality. She's a very gracious lady. I realized it when interviewing her for "Thunderdome," the "Mad Max" movie she made with Mel Gibson. Gibson himself was a forgettable interview, but Tina more than made up for it. She didn't sing in the movie, so, to make up for it, I asked her to sing something during our interview. She did, but it was only a brief bit. Still, it was memorable, and so was she. To my knowledge she hasn't made any more movies, and it's a shame.

Sylvia Miles is another memorable character, and she, too, sang for me during an interview. In this case, it was her idea because the song was from an off-Broadway show she was appearing in at the time. She sang a few bars. I grinned a lot. She finished the song by reaching over and kissing me on the cheek. The surprised look on my face got more attention from television viewers than the interview itself!

Madonna was—and is—my most controversial interview. It wasn't so much what she said about her movie—and I think it was the film "Truth or Dare"—it was the things she said about herself and her costars. The controversy was apparent onscreen when she put two fingers down her throat to simulate throwing up after talking to Kevin Costner. Her comments and body language were even more explicit off-screen during our interview.

I remember her talking about men and women in love. She said men can be happy in love if their women know what really pleases their man—or words to that effect. All I remember is she picked up an empty Coca-Cola bottle and demonstrated oral sex, saying any woman can do it and do it well if she practices.

Madonna also had some choice comments to make about ex-husband Sean Penn ("the only man I really loved!") and about the lack of really good musicals in movies and theater.

She demonstrated her style of dancing in the movie but not in person. I remember she said, "A hotel room interview isn't the place for it."

Madonna likes to shock people, and she does a good job of it. But Shirley MacLaine does it better. The husky-voiced singer-dancer-actress likes to shock people with colorful language. She would combine various salty-sounding adjectives, then watch the faces of those listening. If anyone winced or coughed or even got red-faced, she was encouraged to do more.

"Do you know Bella Abzug?" MacLaine once said, referring to the late political activist.

"No," I replied. "But I know who she is."

"You ought to meet her. You look like her, and that kind of face looks better on you than her. I'll tell her about you the next time I see her, we're fan-f—k—g-tastic good friends," she said. It was the same colorful expletive she used to describe her character's relationship with Jack Nicholson's character in "Terms of Endearment."

Bette Midler is a cheerful interview. I remember how she looked me up and down, smiling all the while, when we were about to do an interview for her film "Beaches."

"You've been to the junkets of all my movies, haven't you?" she asked.

"All except 'Ninja Vixens'," I answered, using the title of a fictitious movie she claimed to have made in the movie, "Outrageous Fortune." She said it when her costar (Shelley Long) was surveying her messy room. She proudly asked if she had seen that movie, and Long cynically answered, "Yes, I'm sure I've seen it."

"You've seen 'Ninja Vixens'?" Midler asked.

Shelley Long was just the opposite of Bette Midler as far as interviews went. She never stopped talking. Not long enough to answer a question.

Olympia Dukakis can be almost as salty-sounding as Shirley MacLaine, and I'm sure that's her aim. They costarred in "Steel Magnolias" and both were at the press junket trying to outcuss each other. Olympia isn't inventive, but she tries harder. Together they shocked the rest of the "Steel Magnolias" cast—Daryl Hannah, Julia Roberts, Sally Field, and Dolly Parton.

Julia Roberts was very shy in those days. She didn't cut loose and become a "personality" until she met and almost married Kiefer Sutherland. They used to walk through the lobby of the hotels where the press junkets were held. They had their arms wrapped around each other and were giggling as they paraded through the lobby. It was shameless showing off, and they knew it. In fact, I think the idea of so much attention is what goaded them on. Sutherland was her first serious boyfriend. He's also the one she stood up at what would have been the wedding of the year.

Olympia Dukakis gave each of her "Steel Magnolias" costars a nickname, but I don't remember them. They were routine names like "Cheerful" and "Blue Eyes." All I remember is that she was delighted with the nickname Shirley MacLaine bestowed on her during the filming of "Steel Magnolias."

"She calls me 'Olympic'!" Olympia would say proudly, and Shirley MacLaine would just beam.

Although I never actually met Barbara Stanwyck, I saw her act in front of the cameras. It was in 1950, when I went home with my college roommate for Thanksgiving in Indianapolis. Barbara Stanwyck and Clark Gable were filming "To Please a Lady" at the Speedway track, and we went to watch them perform, but only Stanwyck was working that day. I saw her up close—her solid gray hair glistening in the Indiana sun. It was exciting to be standing that close to her when she was acting a scene.

During that same time I went to the Indianapolis ice skating arena to see Sonja Henie and her ice show. She skated right up to where I was sitting in the audience and I could feel the spray of ice she caused.

Rosie O'Donnell was another colorful character, but she wasn't as bubbly or as cheerful as she is on television. In fact, she could be downright hostile.

When I interviewed her for "Exit to Eden," she was appearing in a revival of "Grease" on Broadway and I wanted to ask her a question about it.

"What the hell for?" she asked. "I'm here to talk about my movie. I'm not going to waste any words on anything else."

Lana Turner was quite an individual. Some critics I know call her shy. After I met her, I thought she was just plain bad-mannered.

The first time was in California after she made the movie "Bittersweet Love." I was scheduled to meet her for lunch and an interview at the Brown Derby, but her maid called me at the hotel to cancel it.

"I was looking forward to meeting her," I said.

The maid answered, "Well, she has a tummyache and doesn't want to be far away from the bathroom. But she will let you interview her by phone."

I interviewed her on the phone, and it was a very unmemorable talk. She seemed distant and uninterested. She even contradicted her own news reports by insisting she did her own singing in "The Merry Widow" (Trudy Marshall is listed on the Original Soundtrack recording). She also lambasted the press, saying "The press has been very unkind to me. They blame me for things I didn't do and criticize my movies unmercifully."

After lambasting the press, she said bad things about some of her costars and some of her husbands. It was nothing I could really print, so I wrote a comparatively short interview ending with the comment: "Lana Turner—forgotten but not gone!"

Bob Polunsky's Flicker Footnotes

By contrast, Meryl Streep is one of the best interviews I've ever had. She's always upbeat, never insincere, and—most importantly—always has something to say. She is so informative and entertaining that I wanted to give her a big spread in the San Antonio Light when I interviewed her for "A Cry in the Dark." She played a beleaguered wife whose small child is abducted by dingoes (wild dogs) and eaten. Meryl's character was accused of killing the child, and the movie was about the way she fought the accusations.

The press junket was for TV interviews only, but I usually used the same questions for a print interview too. This time it would be a long interview with a particularly good picture of the star in color gracing the printed copy. I was proud of this article but dumbfounded when I got a nasty phone call from her agent.

"You only had permission to do a TV interview," the agent said. "No one granted you permission for a print interview."

"I had it on TV and then put it in print. I thought you'd be happy to get the coverage," I said.

"It's our aim to see that things are done the way they best suit the movie, the star, and our studio system," she said, repeating, "You only had permission to do one interview and it was supposed to be television only."

The next day I called Stu Gottesman at Warner Brothers, and he knew all about the agent's call.

"They like to control things, that's all," he explained. "Actually, all of us at the studio were delighted with your coverage. Don't worry about that agent. She was just feeling her oats."

The next time I saw Meryl Streep, I mentioned the situation. She was completely surprised by it and made sure I knew how much she appreciated the coverage.

Meryl Streep is quite a pro. She always makes sure she knows the interviewer's name and location. I didn't see her ask her assistant for that information, but I did see Kathleen Turner ask. The very sexy-looking Ms. Turner always asked for the name of her next interviewer and where he or she was from. If the interviewer had a Spanish-sounding name, Ms. Turner greeted him or her in Spanish. She had lived in Spain during her youth and had completely mastered the language. She also knew how to communicate better than most interviewees. She never minced words, even if she had to criticize her studio. When I saw her as the fictional detective V.I. Warshawski, I asked if she would film more movies with the character.

"I doubt it," she said. "Not as long as Disney has the rights. They don't spend enough money to do them the way they should be done."

Kathleen Turner is anything but vain. She's just honest. On the other hand, Sharon Stone is completely vain. The press junket for "Basic Instinct," her break-through film, was attended by critics and interviewers from virtually every state in the union. Everyone wanted to get a good look at the sexy actress who made movie history by crossing her legs on camera and revealing her lack of underwear.

Stone knew the interest was there, but she didn't know how to handle it. Although interviewers from all over would question her, no two interviews would likely be shown in the same city. Only the biggest cities had interviewers from more than one TV channel, but Stone insisted on changing clothes between each interview. She redid her hair style slightly as well. She shouldn't have bothered as no one would be able to compare her dress nor appearance. They would talk about her posture, however. She managed to cross her legs suggestively for each interview.

Jodie Foster is a good interview, but she's more reserved than practically any star I've interviewed.

She was particularly shy when I asked her about her movie, "Nell." She answered all questions but there was very little enthusiasm. Only once did she break the pattern of behavior. It was when one of my fellow reporters in the room told her it happened to be my birthday.

"Oh, happy birthday," she said as she got up to leave. She was halfway across the room when she stopped, turned around, rushed back, and planted a kiss on the back of my neck.

"I mean it," she said. "I hope you have a very happy birthday."

I didn't expect a kiss from Jodie Foster, but I would have expected one from Kathy Grant, mainly because I knew her well in college. We dated several times and acted together in Radio House plays at the University of Texas at Austin. She was more active in live theater at the university, but she was never known for her acting. She was chiefly known as a prime example of Texas' homegrown beauty.

We had some classes together before she abruptly left the University to pursue a movie career in Hollywood. She had several flashy roles, chiefly the waitress in the last segment of "Anatomy of a Murder," but her Hollywood fame comes from the fact that she was the second Mrs. Bing Crosby. When she married him, she virtually retired from the mundane Hollywood roles she was handed. To make up for it, she went on tour with various Broadway shows. One of them—and I forget which one—was performed at the Lila Cockrell Theater on the Hemisfair Grounds. My wife and I went backstage after the performance to congratulate Kathy on her acting job. She accepted the congratulations gracefully, then broke the mood by telling me, "Why, Bob, you've really aged."

Carol Channing's comments during our interview were equally surprising but much more charming. She came to San Antonio to headline a production of "Hello, Dolly" at the Majestic Theater, and I taped a TV interview with her in the lobby. Her baby-sounding voice was her most notable trait, and she used it to advantage. I remember her comment whenever she didn't have an answer (or didn't want to answer) one of my questions. She would just turn to the camera and say, "Isn't he cute?"

Lena Horne was much more dramatic. She was very aloof during her early interviews, claiming Hollywood had misused and abused her during her early movie days. It was a lame excuse, as she had enough critical praise and show business success to override her racial-tinged early days. I remember asking her why she made her comeback in the thankless role of the Good Witch in "The Wiz," the movie version of Broadway's all-black "The Wizard of Oz."

"That was pure nepotism, honey," she said. "My son-in-law [Sidney Lumet] made that movie and cast me in it."

Although she was still aloof during our interview, I hit the right nerve when I asked her who she would want to see in a movie about her life. She broke into an approving smile and said, "Well, it's been discussed, and my only stipulation is that I should do my own singing."

Pearl Bailey will probably be the subject of a film biography one day. But—no matter who they get to play her—they won't be able to do her justice. She was a unique personality with a talent to sing and a talent to make people laugh. Although I never went to a press junket to see her, I did get a chance to talk to her on one of her visits to San Antonio. We had a mutual friend—Bobby Sheerin—and Pearl Bailey was the surprise guest at his fiftieth birthday party.

Bobby's wife, Maggie, reserved two private rooms capable of holding two hundred of Bobby's closest friends for a dinner party at the classy St. Anthony Hotel. One room had ice sculptures and every hors d'oeuvre you can possibly think of. The room also had two open bars. Another room was the dining area for the seated dinner. Waiters wearing white gloves served three different meats (beef, pork, lamb) to each guest, plus all the trimmings.

It was a surprise to Bobby, but the biggest surprise was yet to come. During dessert, Maggie took the microphone to tell the guests that Bobby's favorite entertainer was Pearl Bailey and "since I couldn't send all of you to see her, I invited her to see you!"

At that point the curtains on a small stage opened and out stepped Pearl Bailey herself. She sang songs to Bobby and the rest of us for over an hour. At the end of her concert she asked for requests, and Bobby said, "There's something special I'd like." Pearl answered, "I know what you'd like, honey, but I'm too old!" The room rocked with laughter.

When she finished singing, the dinner guests swarmed around her. I was among them but waited till the line thinned out so we could sit down and talk for a few minutes. We talked about her stage shows and movies, since I had seen every movie she ever made as well as her version of "Hello, Dolly" on Broadway.

"If you saw 'Hello, Dolly,' then I'll give you one of my books to show my appreciation," she told me. She handed me one of her many autobiographies—autographed. I was as happy as Bobby Sheerin at that moment.

Marianna Blase was a San Antonio actress who carved a career in community theater with her definitive performance as Amanda in "The Glass Menagerie." It was often requested at the San Antonio Little Theater, and always because Marianna was so good in the role.

Every theater buff in San Antonio knew her, and that includes the moviegoers who saw her in a strong supporting role in Steven Spielberg's first big screen movie, "Sugarland Express." Spielberg filmed the story of a young couple racing across South Texas in an effort to save their son from being adopted by others. Goldie Hawn played the leading female role, but San Antonio's eyes were on Marianna Blase as the "pig lady" on a bus in an important scene.

Marianna also had a colorful supporting role in "Viva Max," a comedy with Peter Ustinov as a Mexican general who marches across Texas to San Antonio to recapture the Alamo. The movie was made in San Antonio. That is, all but the scenes filmed in and around the Alamo itself. The Daughters of the Republic of Texas (custodians of the Alamo) adamantly refused to allow cameras within the hallowed halls of Texas' most famous shrine. A complete replica of the Alamo had to be rebuilt in Italy, where the studio had some frozen funds that couldn't be used outside the country.

But Marianna's role took place in Texas, and she was a delight to watch. I didn't have to request a personal interview since I saw her so often. We had gone to the University of Texas at Austin together, when she was known as Marianna Clore. We were social friends after we both got married, and we often reminisced about some of our classmates—notably, Kathy Grant. Marianna and her husband, Bob, were with us when we went backstage to see Kathy Grant after her performance in San Antonio.

I remember telling Marianna shortly before she died that I'll always think of what she looked like on the stage of Hogg Auditorium in Austin. She was one of my favorite performers, and I had a huge crush on her. I always felt she was a true pro and symbolized everything I thought a movie star should be.

"I fell in love with you and your talent the first time I saw you," I told her.

She had a satisfied smile on her face. "Same back atch ya!" she said. "But don't tell my husband. He's the jealous type."

21.
CAMEOS—THE MEN

MEN IN SHOW BUSINESS AREN'T AS SHOWY OR AS AFFECTED AS THEIR FEMALE counterparts. But some are memorable for a comment or a response here and there.

For the most part, the guys are very down to earth. I could tell that just by watching the passengers come and go at Los Angeles International Airport. It was there that I pulled out my bag from the crowded carousel in the baggage room and accidentally bumped into Vincent Price. He said, "Pardon me, sir," very politely.

"Aren't you Vincent Price?" I asked since I couldn't think of anything else to say at the time.

"Guilty!"

"I'm a great fan of yours."

"Thank you. But would you mind moving your bag so I could get my bag out?"

It was an awkward situation that didn't lend itself to any small talk. But I can say I actually "bumped into" Vincent Price once.

I also bumped into Cary Grant at the LAX airport in a very unusual way. I saw him talking to a couple at the airport and couldn't resist breaking into the conversation. I went up to Grant, grabbed his hand, and said, "Cary! How good it is to see you again!"

He looked completely perplexed but didn't question me. He just shook my hand and said, "Thank you. It's good to see you again too!"

I've seen and met John Lithgow, Ned Beatty, and Christian Slater under similar circumstances at the LAX Airport.

I also saw James Woods driving down Wilshire Boulevard in his convertible. When we both stopped at a stop light, he waved at me.

"Hi! It's Jimmy!" he said. Possibly he recognized me from an interview and possibly not. I'd like to think he did.

Richard Dreyfuss always remembered me from one interview to the next. He said I looked like his cousin Joey, and always addressed me by that name.

Paul Mazursky and I had a long conversation about names. I have relatives named Mazur, and that's similar to Mazursky. The famous director said that probably means we're related.

"The word mazur refers to the marsh people of Russia and Poland," he said. "And the sky at the end of my name just means 'son of,' so I'm the son of marsh people, and you probably are, too."

Spike Lee and I had a conversation about family and relatives, but his attitude was quite different from Paul Mazursky. At one time I told Lee I really admired his movie, "Crooklyn." "I liked the warmth of the characters. They reminded me of my own relatives," I told him.

"That's too bad," he said.

"Why would you say that?"

"Because you're not black."

Spike Lee has probably done more to keep the races stand-offish with one another than anyone else in the country.

Roman Polanski and I also had a brief conversation about our relatives. Too brief, in fact.

It happened at the Beverly Wilshire Hotel in Beverly Hills. I was in the coffee shop with a fellow movie critic when I heard a waiter paging "Mr. Polunsky." I called him over, and he brought a portable phone with him, but the caller wanted "Mr. Polanski," not "Mr. Polunsky."

When I saw the waiter take the phone to Roman Polanski's table, I jumped up and introduced myself to the controversial director.

"Pardon me, but our names are so similar. Could we possibly be related?"

"How do you spell your name," he replied very unceremoniously.

I told him, and he just shook his head and said, "No. I spell my name differently. We're not related."

One of the most unusual interviews I ever had was with bandleader Benny Goodman on a plane between Los Angeles and San Antonio. I had been asked to interview him about his forthcoming concert in the Alamo City. The agent who called said she would make sure we were on the same plane so we could talk, warning me that Mr. Goodman always got to the airport at the last minute.

So I didn't rush. Although I was at the airport early, I didn't go to the gate for a boarding pass right away. I wanted to get my seat assignment when Mr. Goodman came in so we could sit together. When I saw him enter the airport, I introduced myself to him and explained the situation. He was aware of the interview so he promptly got his seat assignment, then turned to me to do the same.

But the agent at the gate said they were overbooked and would have to downgrade me. I raised a little hell over it since it messed up my interview, but Benny Goodman was nice enough to intervene. He got permission to sit with me on the pull-out seats that the stewardesses usually use. He asked for permission to use them for about an hour, and the agent granted it.

Bob Polunsky's Flicker Footnotes

We spoke animatedly for the first hour of the flight, then had a drink together and made small talk for about ten minutes. When I went to my coach seat, he went to his first-class seat. It was a good interview, only there's very little I remember about it now. I just recall him saying that Steve Allen wasn't the right actor to play him in "The Benny Goodman Story."

Bill Murray has always been friendly to me, but I've noticed that he isn't friendly to everyone at press junkets. He's capable of barking out orders and doing exactly what he wants to do, completely ignoring studio rules. He's also a glib talker who isn't above double-talking his way into or out of any situation.

I recall the press junket for "Scrooged" when Murray admired my tie.

"Let's trade ties," he said. "I like yours, and it would look good on me."

"But you're not wearing a tie," I countered.

"And that's exactly why I want yours," he said.

Dan Aykroyd always remembered my name, although "Bob" is all he actually remembers. I've interviewed him at least a half dozen times, and he always greets me by saying, "Hi, Bob."

I remember talking to him at the press junket for "The Blues Brothers" and he graciously came to my defense when I had trouble with his costar, John Belushi.

I wanted an autograph, but Belushi just grunted and walked away.

"Don't worry, I'll handle him," Aykroyd said, as he jumped up and followed Belushi to the next room. In a few minutes he was back with an 8 by 10 still from the movie that was dutifully signed by John Belushi.

Belushi was a tough interview, but, during the interview proper, he answered all questions asked. A really bad interviewee wouldn't answer any question or—in the case of Andrew Dice Clay—he would ridicule the question and the interviewer. Of all the different actors I've interviewed, I've never run across anyone as undisciplined as Andrew Dice Clay.

I met him on the junket for "Ford Fairlane." It was supposed to be his introduction to the big screen but was a major flop. The reason was Clay himself. He would ridicule the speech patterns of all who interviewed him at the junket. He would use the foulest language, thinking he was being funny. But all he did was limit the exposure of the interviews as we couldn't air them with that language and didn't want to air them with the ridiculing comments and exaggerated speech inflection. I remember referring to his movie, "Ford Fairlane." as a lemon with Andrew Dice Clay as the "chief extractor."

Mickey Rooney still acts like the brash teenager he played in the "Andy Hardy" pictures. He's arrogant, spoiled, and egocentric, and I didn't meet him until he was on the downside of his long career.

The first time was for an interview at the theater where he was performing in the revue, "Sugar Babies." He patted himself on the back as he recounted many of his classic films—films like "The Human Comedy," "A Midsummer's Night Dream," "Boys' Town," "Babes in Arms," "Girl Crazy," and the "Andy Hardy" pictures. After listing them proudly, he turned to me and asked, "And what do you think I got out of all those movies playing on television? Absolutely nothing!"

The second time I saw him was at a press junket for the film, "My Heroes Have Always Been Cowboys," in which Rooney played a small part.

He spoke at length about the movies from his youth and once again expressed frustration and self-pity because he didn't get any residuals from their sale to television. He also talked about his several marriages, proudly saying he was the first man to "possess" Ava Gardner (his first wife). It sounded strange because Rooney then lapsed into a long discourse about being a born-again Christian.

Danny Kaye was a fun interview. He would joke a lot, burst into song, and act like an instantaneous showman at all times during the press junket for "The Madwoman of Chaillot" in 1969. He played the Ragpicker in what would be his last theatrical film.

Yul Brynner was colorful when I interviewed him for that same film. He played one of the greedy bad guys in "The Madwoman of Chaillot." The press junket was held in the Bahamas, and "Madwoman" was the last of six films in the Warner Brothers Film Festival that was held there. The studio would show us a different film every night for a week, then take us back to the hotel for a major dinner. The food served was reminiscent of the movie we just saw, so we had French food after seeing "Madwoman of Chaillot."

The films were all big-budget productions, but not all of them were successful in the movie houses nor at the press junket. I recall the most praise going to "The Wild Bunch," the violent western starring William Holden, Ernest Borgnine, and others. We had a big barbecue dinner to celebrate that one. At the time I noticed that Holden needed a script of some kind to show any kind of personality. He was a very bland person.

Several years later I interviewed him for his role in "Network," and someone at the junket asked him why he had left his wife, Brenda Marshall, for one of his costars.

"There comes a time in every man's life when a man gets an instantaneous erection. If he's smart, he'll take full advantage of it," Holden said, in what was the only display of personality I ever saw him deliver in person.

Jack Benny was another star who needed a script. His stock in trade was his sense of comedy timing, but he had to have dialogue written out for him. Benny—like so many show business personalities—came to San Antonio during our Hemisfair World's Fair in 1968. When I met him I foolishly asked him to say something funny.

"I will," he said, "if you write out what you want me to say."

By contrast, Peter Ustinov had a remarkable command of the English language that served him well in every situation. He also had sparkling wit. When I interviewed him at the press junket for Agatha Christie's "Evil

Under the Sun," I told the cameraman to stop me after four minutes as that was long as I could go on the air. I then asked Mr. Ustinov about his role as Hercule Poirot in the movie, and he answered: "I don't have time to explain it in just four minutes."

Since I looked so surprised, he readily added: "I'm only kidding. I got all my information about Poirot from Agatha Christie's descriptions in her books." He then laughed.

Jan Murray used a stockpile of Yiddish phrases to get laughs. He came to San Antonio as a guest performer at our Fiesta Dinner Playhouse. The dinner theater was owned by actor Earl Holliman, and Holliman brought in many big-name stars. Most of them were on the way up or on the way down when they came here. Murray was somewhere in between. We got along great for our interview, and Murray asked me to be a mensch (Yiddish for "man") and take him on a "theater run" to see what the different movie houses looked like. I took him to one of our biggest multiplexes.

"I could spend the day here going from one movie to the next," he said. And he did.

John Malkovich talked about San Antonio with some emotion in his voice. His father had been killed in San Antonio in an accident some years earlier.

Steve Guttenberg had a press junket in Dallas but he wanted to see San Antonio. He came down, and—while here—wanted to see the video store my wife and I owned. We specialized in "hard-to-find" movies and Guttenberg said, "Can you get me a copy of 'Bad Medicine'? It's one of my earlier movies and I can't find it anywhere."

My wife and I found the tape for him.

Steven Spielberg and I had a nice long chat about the filming of "Sugarland Express."

"You refer to Sugarland, Texas, and it's in the flat lands around Houston," I said. "But you showed it in the Hill Country around San Antonio in your movie."

"I never said Sugarland was in the Hill Country," he replied. "I just photographed the Hill Country because it looks good on the screen!"

Spielberg was friendly enough to remember me on successive visits. I happened to be in Hollywood when the Disney studio was having a big Christmas Party at the Buena Vista Studios in Burbank one year. They invited celebrities and their families, and Steven Spielberg and his then-wife Amy Irving were included. He remembered me from a junket and asked if he could "double date" with Paulina and me for the Disney party.

James Caan was always an interesting interview. He acts much like he acts onscreen and for pretty much the same reason: He rarely if ever rehearses a scene before filming it. It's the same with his interviews. He prides himself on it, even though his attitude has lost him some jobs. One in particular was the movie, "Dad." Caan was signed to play Jack Lemmon's son but refused to rehearse. Ted Danson replaced him.

Danny Glover is a friendly guy. Once he meets you and likes you, he greets you with a bear hug. It's an endearing trait but can come as a surprise when he sees you in a crowded room.

By contrast, Samuel L. Jackson is quite formal, even after several meetings. He always called me "Mister," while I called him "Sam."

John Cusack and Johnny Depp are typical of the "New Wave" of young stars during the 1990s. Both brag about it to the point of proudly telling interviewers how they trashed their hotel rooms.

Jack Lemmon is an intellectual interview while his frequent costar, Walter Matthau, is a self-mocking comedian. The only really serious comment Matthau made to me was that he thought Jack Lemmon was "the finest actor working in Hollywood today." Lemmon's most light-hearted comment was that "Walter Matthau is my favorite leading lady!"

Pat O'Brien always reminded me of my father. He looked so much like him that I adopted O'Brien as a father-figure. That's why I was happy to hear that he would be in San Antonio performing in "On Golden Pond" at the Fiesta Dinner Playhouse.

I got permission to interview him backstage after the show. I also got permission to take my mother with me, and she was the first to tell him that he and my father were look-alikes.

"Oh, the poor fellow," O'Brien said, then laughed out loud. It was one of the friendliest interviews I ever had.

Roddy MacDowell came to the Fiesta Playhouse to play the lead in "Harvey." His birthday was September 17, and that happens to be my wife's birthday, too. I took her to the play, and she had a delightful time interviewing Roddy afterwards.

Paulina substituted for me at times. Once she talked to John Howard when I couldn't be there. He was the only surviving member of the cast of "Lost Horizon" when it was reissued in the 1980s.

Paulina went to New York to interview Christopher Reeve, Eddie Murphy, and Christopher Lambert. She went to Hollywood to interview Robin Williams, Chris Farley, and David Spade. All were exceptionally good interviews. Paulina wouldn't have them any other way.

I also sent my daughter, Julianne, to cover for me, and the studio went along with it without question because they wanted the San Antonio market covered.

She interviewed David Keith, star of "The Lords of Discipline," a film based on the Pat Conroy novel by director Franc Roddam. Roddam asked Julie to go out with him and she had dinner with him along with a staff of Hollywood people.

Paul Newman was an unpredictable interview. When I talked to him about "Slap Shot" he said, "I'd rather have a beer with you than talk about me." When I complimented him on "The Verdict," he shook my hand and said, "Thanks for that. I appreciate it."

Robert Morley was a colorful interview. I recall waiting to go into his room when the door opened and he ran out. "There's a woman in there who told me I'm not fat!" he said, patting his oversized belly. He then looked at my oversized belly and said, "I wouldn't go in there if I were you!"

Tom Cruise was an unspoiled young actor when he started out. I spoke to him at the press junket for "Taps," the military-school melodrama in which he played the villain. He was always smiling, very cooperative, and friendly. For that matter so was his costar, Sean Penn.

Cruise changed when he became a top box office player. I talked to him to publicize "Far and Away" and "Days of Thunder," and he was friendly enough, but his attitude changed at the junket for "A Few Good Men." His agent issued a letter stating that Cruise would only talk to critics from the nation's top ten markets. That left me out. It also left out most of the junketing press, but the critics from New York and Los Angeles qualified.

After the movie, my wife got into an elevator and lo and behold, Tom Cruise was in it. She said, "I enjoyed your movie, Mr. Cruise," and he thanked her. When the elevator stopped, he motioned for her to walk out first. She shook her head and stepped back.

"Aren't you getting out at our interview floor?" he asked her.

"No, but you are," she replied.

Sean Penn also became "too hot to handle" for ordinary interviewers as his fame became more pronounced. He rarely consented to interviews but made an exception with "Colors," the police melodrama directed by his friend, Dennis Hopper.

In the context of our interview, I asked Penn if he would make more films with his then-wife, Madonna. They had recently costarred in "Shanghai Surprise," and it bombed big-time.

He paused for a time before answering and glowered at me. He obviously resented the question but he dutifully answered it: "We would have to give it careful consideration first," he said.

Robin Williams is an erratic interview. He never sits still and doesn't answer all questions. He makes faces and noises and gets so animated all he and his interviewer can do is laugh.

I remember his asking me where I was from. "Texas" was my reply and he said, "Oh, Tex-iz" in a mock western drawl. He conducted the rest of the interview with the same drawl but never mocked me like Andrew Dice Clay did. He didn't have much suitable material either. The movie was "Good Morning, Vietnam," and he interrupted himself several times to "announce" the title of his movie. The only answer I remember was when I asked him about his experience filming "Popeye," and he said, "I'll make a sequel to 'Popeye' when I learn to keep the other eye closed."

Bob Polunsky

I've always been a fan of Fred Astaire and Gene Kelly and have had the opportunity to interview both.

Astaire was, for the most part, a perfect gentleman and answered every question in detail. The interview was for "Ghost Story," one of his few non-dancing films, and I recall asking him about his various dancing partners. He didn't criticize any or make light of any of them, but he did give glowing reviews to Rita Hayworth and Cyd Charisse so they were obviously his favorites. He never mentioned Ginger Rogers, even though she made more movies with him than any of his other partners.

Gene Kelly was not a gentleman. He was more of a cynic, making detrimental comments about Astaire and boasting about himself. I talked to him when he was on the decline. He had just finished making "That's Dancing," his next-to-last film. (He made "That's Entertainment III" shortly afterward.)

Kelly spoke of himself as an innovator and one of the "most honored dancers in movie musical history." I've no doubt that it was true, but he wouldn't have won a public relations citation of any kind. According to him, he danced because it was his work and Astaire danced because he considered dancing a form of play. My illusions about the great Gene Kelly were shattered by that interview.

John Goodman was a fun interview, but not because he was very informative. I talked to him to publicize "Babe," in which he played Babe Ruth, and he supplied good answers. But he wanted to end the interview on an upbeat note and asked if he could repeat his characterization from "C.H.U.D." (which stands for "Cannibalistic Humanoid Underground Dwellers"), a low-budget horror film he made early in his career.

"Well, the camera first focuses on me when I see the cannibal monsters coming toward me. My instructions were to register complete horror, so I turned my head away, then slowly turned it back, opened my mouth, and let out a scream!" He then screamed, bringing a noisy end to our interview.

22.
I'll Always Remember "Pearl Harbor"

THE PRESS JUNKET FOR THE MOVIE "PEARL HARBOR" WAS THE LAST MAJOR junket I attended. It may be the last one I'll ever attend, because an accident during the junket left me somewhat crippled. But it was a junket I really wanted to attend.

The junket was held in May 2001, at Pearl Harbor itself in Honolulu. All interviews would be aboard an aircraft carrier, and all press representatives would be invited to the gala World Premiere aboard the ship at the end of the week-long junket. But not their wives and families. We could bring them (at our own expense), but there would be no security clearance for them so they could not take part in the military proceedings.

It didn't matter. I wanted to take Paulina and Stephanie, the seven-year-old grandaughter we were raising. We went to Hawaii together, and Paulina and Stephanie spent their days on the beach or in the Sheraton Waikiki Hotel swimming pool. I spent my days aboard the aircraft carrier and, later, in the computer room to send my interviews back to the newspaper at home.

The list of stars was impressive. The main ones were Ben Affleck, Josh Hartnett, and Kate Beckinsale. They were the principal players, and all three were involved in a tragic love affair in the film.

Affleck and Hartnett played two lifelong friends who grew up together. Affleck confides to Hartnett that he's fallen in love with a British nurse (Beckinsale) and plans to marry her. But first he is going to fulfill his lifelong dream of fighting with the R.A.F. in England.

Kate tries to talk him out of it, but his mind is made up. Then, in England, he's in an accident at sea and reported dead. Kate is inconsolable, but Josh helps her forget by promptly falling in love with her himself.

Ben escapes England and goes back to Hawaii, only to discover that his girlfriend and his best friend are lovers. They have a bitter fight, but the attack on Pearl Harbor brings them together again.

The forty-minute attack scene is the highlight of the movie and is brilliantly done. The love story disappointed many moviegoers, especially younger ones used to a more melodramatic and sexy love story in modern-day movies.

For my part, I felt the love story was dramatized much like the love stories that came out during World War II. It was realistic for its time period in movie history. But I was probably the only member of the junketing press—and they came from all over the world, including Japan—who liked the movie the way it was.

I rushed around like mad in the computer room with print articles defending my view by describing the action of the movie and the acting by the stars. I rushed so much, I fell and hit my knee against a solid steel doorstop attached to one of the doors.

My knee hurt like hell and—in a matter of minutes—my kneecap was swollen with a bruised, purple covering over it. I thought it would pass and didn't stop to see a doctor at the time. I still had most of the week's junketeering left, with interviews with all the major cast members except Jon Voight (he played FDR in the film). Voight was on location with another film and couldn't make it. But Affleck, Hartnett, Beckinsale, Dan Aykroyd, Tom Sizemore, James King (a woman and a darned pretty one at that), Alec Baldwin, director Michael Bay, and producer Jerry Bruckheimer were there, and I didn't miss talking to any of them.

At one point one of the studio reps got me a cane to use when climbing the stairs aboard the aircraft carrier. It helped, but the swelling didn't go down and there wasn't a doctor I could see at the hotel. Not until the last day of the junket anyway, and he told me I had chipped my kneecap and torn a ligament. It was serious only because I didn't get medical attention right away, and it hurt when I walked and when I sat down. But it wasn't unbearable, so I went to the gala premiere but didn't stay for the party afterwards. I had run out of codeine tablets for the pain by then.

The premiere was a flashy affair with the Honolulu Symphony on the stage before the film started. They played thundering overtures that were punctuated by fireworks across the sky to simulate "bombs bursting in air." The symphony also played the anthems of the Army, Navy, and Air Force. Members of each branch stood in the audience to sing their anthems, and Faith Hill was onstage to sing "The Star Spangled Banner."

Red carpets had been laid out for all the stars as they came aboard the ship and—like my counterparts—I had a microphone to greet each and every one of them with a brief interview. This included Cuba Gooding Jr., who had not attended the regular interview session. These brief interviews—the stars of the movie, a few visiting celebrities, director Bay, and producer Bruckheimer—were used as teasers on the day of the review on TV.

My review was scheduled between 8:00 and 9:00 A.M. on the Friday that the film opened. I then talked to the producers of the other morning news shows and asked them to run my full-length TV interviews. I had three of them—one with star Ben Affleck, one with the security people who saw to it that everything in the film was historically accurate, and one with Bruckheimer. The producers gave me the days they would run, but rearranged them without telling me and I had advised my Disney rep of the dates. The rep had a monitoring service check, and couldn't find them.

I thought I had it all covered when I gave her the rescheduled dates, but the producers skipped the interview with the government security people because they didn't think the security people had done a good job. That much was true. The film was filled with inaccuracies, but they should have advised me of the cancellation. As it was, it got me in trouble with my rep.

Of the three, the interview with Bruckheimer was the best. He was up front about everything, talking about his arguments with the studio about the budget and the editing process used to re-create the actual attack on Pearl Harbor.

Affleck's interview was okay, but it was obvious that he had memorized enough information to answer almost any possible question about the film and his character. That in itself would be okay, but Affleck recited the information so it was obvious that he had memorized it.

I talked to him about the brief basic training that he and Josh Hartnett attended to prepare themselves for military life as pictured in the film. I also asked if the storyline matched the information he must have studied in school. He gave satisfactory answers but didn't show much enthusiasm for the interview or the movie.

I later heard that he acted that way with everyone who interviewed him. His costar, Josh Hartnett, proved to be a much livelier interview. He spoke at length about his love scene with Kate Beckinsale and described how he guided her into the simulated sex act. It was a surprising comment, but Beckinsale confirmed it. She said, "Josh just told me to relax."

Dan Aykroyd was—as usual—an enjoyable interview. He remembered my first name and used it often during the interview. He also described himself as a history buff and confirmed the fact that the political things presented in the movie really happened. After the film was released, various groups insisted that things were exaggerated. The critics were extremely hostile to the idea of placating the Japanese by indicating they didn't really want to attack Pearl Harbor but were forced to it because of the economics of the time.

Tom Sizemore—a self-proclaimed macho guy—talked more about sports than his role in the film. He played a gung-ho sailor aboard the ship and played it well. I realized after talking to him that he was really playing himself.

The studio recruited several survivors from Pearl Harbor, and they attended press junkets as well as the gala World Premiere. Some were in wheelchairs, others on crutches, and some actually walked around under their own power. Each was extremely proud to be associated with the movie as well as with the real-life event it commemorated.

I got through the interviews, the premiere, and the long homeward flight with the help of codeine tablets and lots of squirming. Once I was home in San Antonio I saw a doctor who confirmed the chipped kneecap and torn ligament. He also said there was nothing that could really be done about them and I'd just have to live with them.

The upshot is that my "injuries" gave me a reason to remember "Pearl Harbor." It was not only the most impressive press junket I'd ever attended, but also one of the most controversial. Some people literally hated the movie, calling it "unrealistic" and unbearably talky and hokey. I didn't agree, and my review in the newspaper, radio, and TV said why. I got more mail and more phone calls than I had received for any other review or interview, and that much was heartening. Whether the people agreed with me or disagreed was immaterial. They read it, listened to it, and watched it. It was all a critic could ask for, and "Pearl Harbor" was a fitting climax to the sort of thing I've loved doing for fifty years.